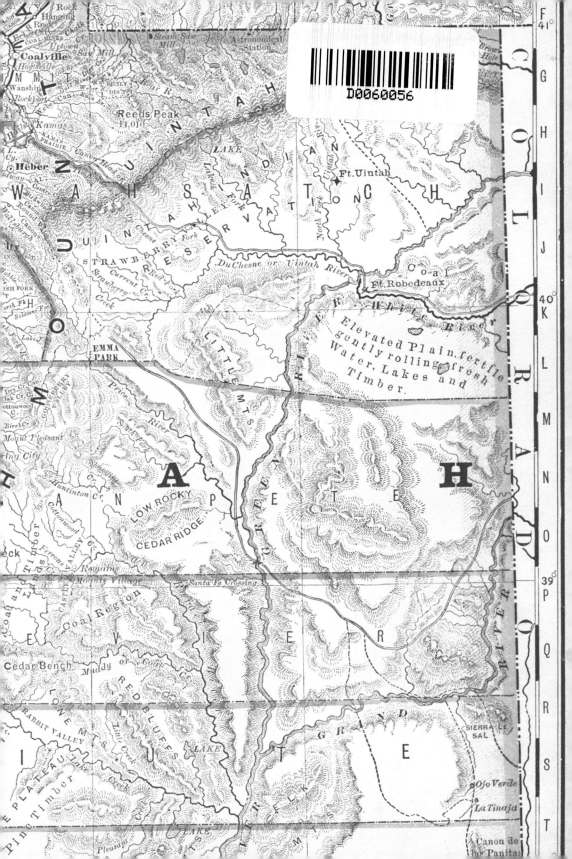

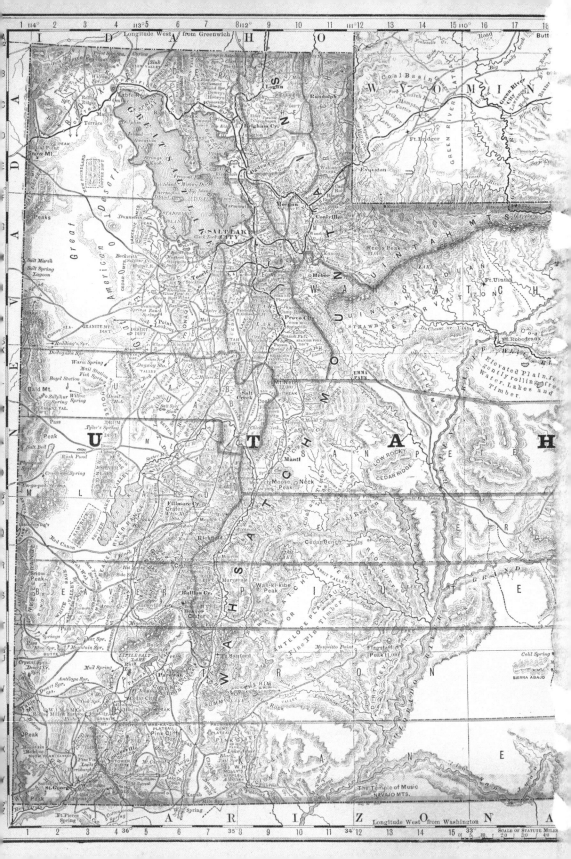

Stories from the Life of

Porter Rockwell

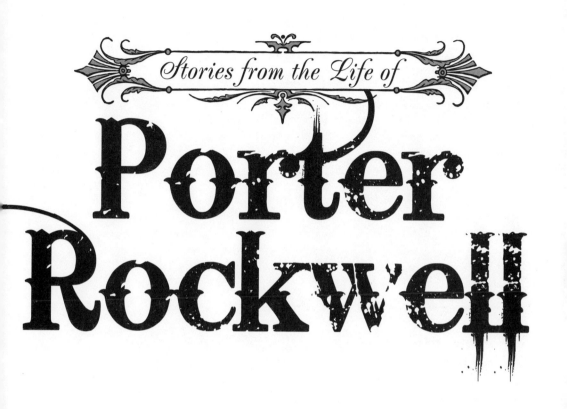

Stories from the Life of Porter Rockwell

JOHN W. ROCKWELL &
JERRY BORROWMAN

Covenant Communications, Inc.

Cover: Orrin Porter Rockwell by Ken Corbett © Draper Visual Arts Foundation
www.drapervisualarts.org, Utah Map Courtesy of www.istockphoto.com

Endsheets: Utah Map Courtesy of www.istockphoto.com

Interior Images:
pg xxxvi–xxxvii *One Last Look at Fair Nauvoo* by Harold I. Hopkinson.

pg 90–91 *Ambushed at the Watering Hole* © Clark Kelly Price. For more information please visit
www.clarkkelleyprice.com.

pg 128–129 *Dead or Alive* © Clark Kelly Price. For more information please visit
www.clarkkelleyprice.com.

Interior ink drawings © Sarah Swanson. For more information please visit
http://www.wix.com/SarahSwanson/Sarah-Illustration

Cover and Interior design © 2010 by Covenant Communications, Inc.

Published by Covenant Communications, Inc.
American Fork, Utah

Printed in Canada
First Printing: May 2010

16 15 14 13 12 11 10   10 9 8 7 6 5 4 3 2 1

ISBN 978-1-60861-005-1

TABLE OF CONTENTS

Preface.. xi

Introduction.. xv

Images.. xxi

PORTER AND JOSEPH

A Cry in the Night 1

Shared Adversity.. 5

Can't I Stay Up and Keep the Pine Torch Lit?........... 7

Treasure Hunting 9

Porter's Ferry—The Turning Point........................ 11

A Trail of Sorrow—Jackson, Clay, and Caldwell 17

Porter and the Danites.. 21

The Missouri War... 27

Attempted Escape from Liberty Jail 29

Porter and Joseph in Washington DC.................... 35

Attempted Assassination of Governor Boggs........... 39

Porter on the Lam 45

Porter and the Jailbreak 49

Porter Goes Fishing While in Jail.......................... 53

Plots and Treason 57

Joseph Prophesies for Porter 61

Alexander Donovan Defends Porter 63

Porter's Dramatic Entrance and Blessing...................................67

Porter's First Saloon—The Mansion House 69

The *Nauvoo Expositor*...71

If My Life Has No Value to My Friends 73

Carthage 77

Porter's Revenge 81

You Throw Rocks—I'll Throw Lead 83

Porter Is Endowed 85

Porter's New Calling...87

PORTER IN THE WEST

Porter on His Own..93

Porter in the Vanguard 95

Early Days in Utah..99

Porter in California 103

Porter Cuts His Hair 109

The Utah Mormon War..113

Harassing Johnston's Army 119

The Aiken Brothers 123

PORTER AND THE OUTLAWS

Porter Rockwell—Territorial Deputy Marshal 131

    Porter at Camp Floyd 131

    The Case of the Great Bullion Robbery 131

    The Bear River Massacre..133

    The Chauncey Millard Incident.................................135

Porter and the Horse Thieves...139

    Lot Huntington 139

Stolen Mules and Horses 140

Shoot First and Then Invite Them In 142

Porter and the Gunslingers...145

Shootout on Lehi State Street..145

California Gunslingers 146

Porter and Oates 146

Joe Dorton and the Tongue of Flame............................147

Tall Tales 149

The McRae Brothers..150

Family, Prayer, and Healing...153

Porter As a Businessman..157

Porter's Last Day...161

Afterword..165

PREFACE

After Porter Rockwell's death, his last wife, Christine Olsen, received a patriarchal blessing. She was concerned about her husband's spiritual welfare, but in the blessing the patriarch announced to her that God would pass by all of her husband's faults because of the many times that he saved the Prophet Joseph's life.

As a young man in 1968, I was called to serve a mission to Mexico. This is still when general authorities were assigned to set missionaries apart for their missions rather than stake presidents. My family and I traveled to Salt Lake City to the Church Administration Building, where we met with Elder Theodore M. Burton, a member of the Quorum of the Seventy. Upon shaking my hand, he asked me if I was a descendant of Orrin Porter Rockwell, to which I answered in the affirmative. I told him that my father was the great-grandson of Porter, and I was his great-great-grandson. This spiritual leader shook my hand firmly and said to me, "Be proud of your ancestry for the many times that your great-great-grandfather saved the life of the Prophet Joseph Smith." That is something that has always stayed with me.

It reminds me of a story that occurred in Nauvoo in 1844. As the mayor of Nauvoo, Joseph Smith ordered the arrest of Augustine Spencer for assaulting his own brother, Orson Spencer. Porter and Joseph were with the city marshal, J.P. Greene, as he attempted to arrest Spencer. Also present were three sworn enemies of Joseph Smith: Chauncey Higbee and the two Foster brothers, Robert and Charles, who intervened to prevent the arrest. They started shouting and cursing at Joseph.

With his patience exhausted, Joseph ordered the marshal to arrest Higbee and the Foster brothers as well. Instead, the sheriff ordered them to leave, which they refused to do, continuing their verbal abuse against Joseph. Joseph lost his temper and grabbed the two Foster brothers and slammed them against a wall. Charles Foster quickly drew a pistol from his coat and took aim at the Prophet. Just as he was firing, Porter jumped between Joseph and Foster and knocked the pistol from Foster's hand. Foster cursed and screamed at Joseph, saying, "I would have killed you. I would be favored of God for the privilege of ridding the world of such a tyrant." But he was thwarted in the attempt by Porter Rockwell, who might well have lost his own life in trying to save Joseph's.

In the end, the three men were arrested and fined $100 each for the assault upon Joseph Smith. True to Joseph's forgiving nature, he tried in vain to amend the difficulties he had with these adversaries. This is just one example of many of the times that Porter saved the life of the Prophet Joseph.[1]

Not long after the incident with the Higbee brothers, Porter chanced to see Chauncey Higbee at a hotel. Higbee unfortunately made an insulting remark to Porter about Joseph Smith, and true to Porter's character, he beat the man senseless. When Joseph Smith got word of what had happened, he said quietly that Porter had done "nobly as a friend ought to do."[2]

In this book we have quoted both critics and admirers of Porter Rockwell. Our goal is to help the reader capture a sense of the man and the times in which he lived based on the stories told of him. Because he never learned to read or write, we have no firsthand accounts to refer to and so must rely on journal entries and histories. The tales they tell are fascinating and sometimes disturbing. But whatever else you think of Porter

---

1 For reference, see the newspaper *Nauvoo Neighbor,* May 1, 1844, and also Harold Schindler. *Orrin Porter Rockwell, Man of God/ Son of Thunder.* (Salt Lake City, Utah: University of Utah Press, 1993). 1st ed., 118–19.

2 *History of the Church* 6:414.

Rockwell, honesty requires that he be acknowledged as a friend and protector of Joseph Smith, whom I believe to be a prophet. That is one of the many reasons why I am proud and grateful to be descended from a man such as Orrin Porter Rockwell.

—John W. Rockwell

INTRODUCTION

IN ITS FIRST EDITION AFTER Orrin Porter Rockwell's fatal heart attack in 1878, the *Salt Lake Tribune*—then a virulently anti-Mormon newspaper—ran the headline "Porter Rockwell the Chief of the Danite Band Shuffles Off in a Stable—and Cheats the Hangman of a Worthy Candidate." The editorial then spoke of the despicable acts he had committed in his life, including participation in "at least a hundred murders for the Church, none of which he ever divulged." This leaves little doubt as to what they thought of Porter Rockwell.

At Porter's funeral a few days later, the young Apostle Joseph F. Smith, son of Hyrum Smith and nephew of the Prophet Joseph Smith, painted a very different picture of Porter when he said, "He had his little faults, but Porter's life on earth, taken altogether, was one worthy of example, and reflected honor upon the Church. Through all the trials he has never once forgotten his obligations to his brethren and his God."

As has so often been the case in Porter Rockwell's history, his critics tried to get the final word when the *Salt Lake Tribune* then commented on Elder Smith's eulogy by writing, "A fitting tribute from one outlaw to the memory of another. . . ."

And so we face the central question of Porter Rockwell's life: what should we believe? Do we accept the judgment of Rockwell's numerous critics and enemies, or do we listen to the prophets and apostles who admired him, trusted him, and relied on him as their protector and loyal friend? Should we rely on accounts from the Saints whose lives were saved or improved by Porter Rockwell? Or should we base our opinion on the sensational accounts from the Eastern newspapers of the day about the evil empire created by Brigham Young and his cohorts in the lawless West? Ultimately, was Porter Rockwell a "destroying angel" or a guardian angel?

Porter Rockwell at times resorted to violence. We know of approximately twenty-four men who lost their lives to his gun. In the majority of these instances, he was bringing outlaws to justice in his lawfully appointed role as deputy marshal. In other cases he was defending his own life. After dispatching his would-be murderers, Rockwell always dutifully turned himself in to be tried in the appropriate court of law. For each of these trials he was exonerated as having acted in self-defense. In the most notorious case to haunt him, the shooting of former Governor Lilburn Boggs, a jury of non-Mormons acquitted him, even though strongly prejudiced against the Mormons.

Even when justified, Rockwell's scuffles sometimes seem out of harmony with our modern sense of how a Latter-day Saint should behave. Some members of the Church seem embarrassed by Porter Rockwell, as if his notoriety is out of character with the way the early Church should be portrayed. Hostile nonmembers are more brazen and use the myths that surround his life to discredit the early Church and its leaders.

After all, Porter Rockwell was connected to the founding of the Church since the beginning. As the ninth person to be baptized into the Church on April 6, 1830, no one was more directly involved in the growth of the Church in its infancy than Porter Rockwell, and the life he led was crucial to its survival. Porter was the man who rowed Joseph Smith across the river on the night that he hoped to find refuge in the West, and it was Porter who rowed him back across the river to face his death at Carthage. It was Porter who served as the lead scout for the original Brigham Young wagon train when it first entered the Great Salt Lake valley. Porter was one of those who successfully harassed the invading Johnston's army, slowing their arrival to the outskirts of Salt Lake City long enough that the residents could abandon their homes in preparation for a final war. These are just a handful of the meaningful moments that Porter Rockwell participated in throughout the early history of the Church.

Porter Rockwell was a man of action. He could be up and in the saddle at a moment's notice if Joseph Smith or Brigham Young needed him. In doing so, he influenced the course of history. These and other important stories prove the value of chronicling Porter Rockwell's life.

Accounts have already been written with well-documented biographies and entries in *History of the Church*. Porter's life has even been fictionalized, both in his own day and in more recent years, with words attributed to him that he never really spoke. In fact, very few of his words are recorded, since Porter was unable to read or write. Thus, everything known of him comes from the accounts of others.

Stories from the Life of Porter Rockwell is not another biography, nor is it fiction. It is not intended as a history of the Church in the 1800s. Our goals are simpler than either of those—we simply want to repeat for contemporary readers some of the stories about Porter Rockwell that provide insight into his character, his incredible physical strength and skill, and his devotion to the restored gospel of Jesus Christ. Perhaps by reading these stories, you will find a connection to and appreciation for the unbelievable sacrifices the early members of the Church made in order to become a Saint. In the end, if you believe that men like Brigham Young, Joseph Smith, and Joseph F. Smith were truthful in their judgment, then you must accept that Porter Rockwell was one of those saints of the early latter days.

Even though this is not a biography, some biographical information will help the reader understand the stories found in this book.

Although more than seven years younger than Joseph Smith, Porter Rockwell was great friends with Joseph from childhood.

For example, Porter told Joseph Smith III after his father's death that "they have killed the only friend I have." Joseph Smith had no more loyal and devoted friend and defender than Porter Rockwell. He depended on him for his life.

Porter was extremely skilled in handling firearms. After his home was literally torn apart by mobs (the roof, the walls, and the floorboards torn apart by marauders on horseback while his terrified wife stood looking on), Porter resolved that he would never be unarmed again, and he went into the woods to practice his shooting skills until no one was his equal with a weapon.

He was relatively short—5'6" tall, which was ordinary for the day even though short by today's standards. He was very powerfully built with muscular arms and chest. Porter wore his hair and beard long and uncut for a reason. After a very difficult imprisonment on false charges, Joseph Smith blessed him that as long as he didn't cut his hair, no bullet or knife could harm him. Porter believed this to be a literal blessing, which he put to the test on numerous occasions. That is why he is often called a "modern-day Sampson."

Porter had a gift for animal husbandry. He was as much at ease in the saddle as he was in the driver's seat controlling a team of horses pulling a wagon. This skill would serve the Saints well as he crisscrossed the plains on their behalf between Nebraska and Salt Lake City.

He was not a polygamist, although he was married to three women at different points in his life. He loved his family and provided well for them.

He was not intimidated by authorities who falsely accused him or Mormons. On one occasion he was in the audience while United States Vice President Schuyler Colfax was speaking. When Colfax berated the Mormons for harboring "that murderer Porter Rockwell," Rockwell spoke up from the crowd and said very clearly, "I never killed any man who didn't deserve it." The vice president was so unnerved by this that he ended his speech early and quickly left town. It was clear that Porter acted out of conviction and a sense of right and wrong.

Porter Rockwell was a successful businessman and rancher. At his death he was one of the wealthiest men in Utah, although whatever wealth he actually possessed has not endured. He operated saloons and hotels, livery services, and mail operations, among other ventures.

He also drank liquor, since the expectations of his day were different than ours, and many Church members consumed alcohol. No one in his day looked down on Porter for owning taverns. In fact, some of our most interesting stories will talk about that.

A highly respected deputy marshal, Rockwell brought order to even the most chaotic situations. Sometimes this necessitated shooting criminals—a very serious matter. There is not a known record depicting Rockwell's feelings about this or whether he felt guilty. There is nothing to suggest that Porter Rockwell killed out of passion, revenge, or even anger. He wasn't the type of man to walk into a saloon and start shooting up the place. In most instances he gave the offender a chance to surrender and come back to jail, unless Porter was defending himself, in which case he fired first and asked questions later. The image of Porter as an out-of-control murderer, as portrayed by some of his critics, is simply not supported by the record. Extreme control is a better description. When he entered a situation that required force—even deadly force—he sized things up and acted immediately to bring the situation under control.

Because the historical record is incomplete, this book does not seek to justify Porter Rockwell. There is much to admire in Porter Rockwell. There are also events that make us uncomfortable. However, what is known of Porter Rockwell's life speaks for itself—portraying the man as a legend from our history.

IMAGES

First known photo of Orrin Porter Rockwell

By Darrell High

Site of the Rockwell Farm north of Manchester near the Smith home and farm.

Early Nauvoo—Rockwells' home is in the center with the white window.

Courtesy John W. Rockwell

Nauvoo Mansion House.

Courtesy John W. Rockwell

Stage of Nauvoo Social Hall where Porter tried his hand at acting.

Rendering of Hot Springs Brewery Hotel and Pony Express station owned by Porter, near the point of the mountain.

Stable at Hot Springs Brewery Hotel circa 1858.

Courtesy Utah State Historical Society

Stable at Hot Springs Brewery Hotel circa 1923.

Courtesy John W. Rockwell

Site of the Hot Springs Brewery Hotel.

Courtesy John W. Rockwell

Rockwell Ranch in Skull Valley.

Courtesy Albert M. Cook

Rockwell Ranch in Skull Valley prior to 1982.

Courtesy Albert M. Cook

Rockwell Ranch in Skull Valley.

Courtesy John W. Rockwell

Government Creek at Rockwell Ranch, Skull Valley.

Porter circa 1855 with hair combed back and braided.

Courtesy Joe Nardone, Pony Express Trails Association

Painting of Indian Ford on the Jordan River, where Porter once had a ferry.

Courtesy Audrey Swensen

Rockwell Cabin at Cherry Creek Ranch.

Returning from Battle of Bear River, by Lynn Fausett. Porter is the one raising his hat.

State Street, Lehi 1873. Far right corner is the site of the shootout with Warren Dibble.

Porter in his mid-fifties
Courtesy Church Archives
Church of Jesus Christ of Latter-day Saints

Porter, taken just before his death in 1878.

Courtesy LDS Church Archive

Where Porter died, Colorado Stables, owned by Porter Rockwell in Salt Lake City on State Street and Broadway.

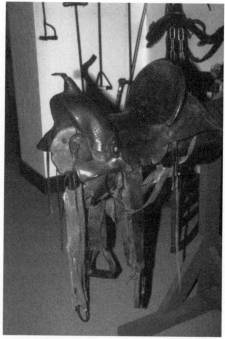

Statue of Rockwell by Stanley Wanlass.

Rockwell's saddle in the John Hutchings Museum.

Above: Porter's 1860 Army Colt

Courtesy Utah State Historical Society

Below left and right: Porter's cane given to him by Joseph Smith.

Courtesy John W. Rockwell

Courtesy Utah State Historical Society

Old Rockwell Monument commemorating Pony Express station.

Courtesy John W. Rockwell

Courtesy John W. Rockwell

Current Rockwell Pony Express Station Monument.

Right above and below: Rockwell's gravesite in the Salt Lake City Cemetery.

Courtesy John W. Rockwell

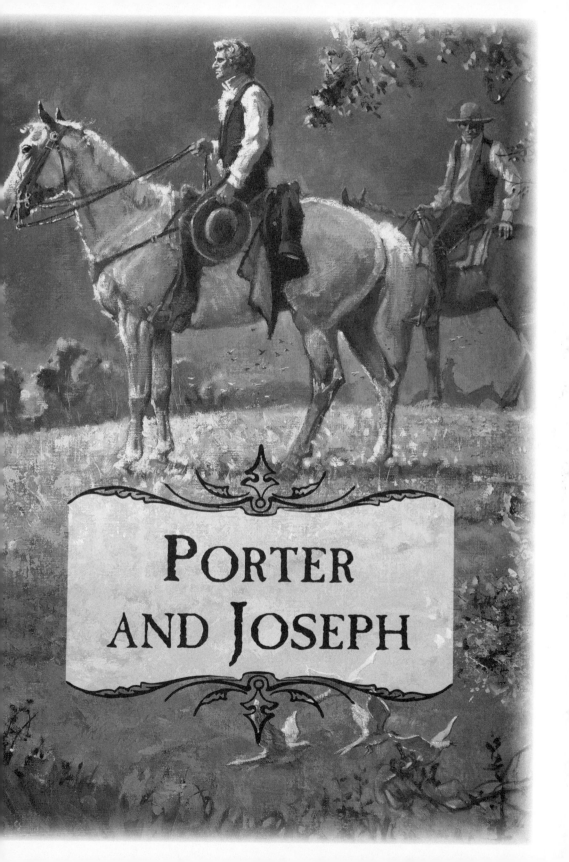

PORTER AND JOSEPH

A Cry in the Night

"THEY'VE KILLED HIM! THEY'VE KILLED JOSEPH!"
The voice crying out in the night was at first unrecognizable to the startled citizens of Nauvoo, Illinois, on this sultry summer night of June 27, 1844.

"They've killed him . . ."

The sound, now farther away as the rider made his way up and down the village streets, betrayed an overwhelming sense of despair mingled with righteous fury and indignation.

"It's Old Port," said a witness to the event, electrified by the news the man was shouting. If it was Porter Rockwell, then the news must be true. He was, after all, the Prophet's personal bodyguard.

But how could it be true? Joseph Smith the Prophet had so many times before been taken by his enemies, only to escape and return to the Saints. Why should this time be different? Even Emma Smith had prevailed on her husband to face his accusers, confident that Governor Ford would live up to his promise to protect Joseph while in the custody of the state.

But of course it was true, as evidenced by the messenger whose voice still rang out in the distance—now far down by the Mississippi River itself, the very place where the night before Joseph, Hyrum, and Willard Richards had successfully made their way to the Iowa shore, where the freedom and safety of the West awaited them. Porter Rockwell, Joseph's friend from childhood, had rowed the three Church leaders across the river and out of the clutches of their enemies. But then an appeal from Joseph's wife, Emma, delivered to Joseph by Porter as well as Reynolds Cahoon had persuaded the Prophet that he must either return to Illinois or be branded a coward. Before their return crossing, Joseph had told Porter in confidence that this next imprisonment would be fatal, but when others heard this, few believed it.

One of the great sorrows of Porter's life in the years that followed was that Joseph had ordered him to turn back to Nauvoo while on the way to Carthage. Porter had protested that it was his job to be there with Joseph and Hyrum Smith, John Taylor, and Willard Richards to protect them. Certainly no one in the struggling young Church was better suited to that than Porter Rockwell, for he was a crack shot and Joseph Smith's fearless defender. But Joseph had told him to leave them and go back, and Porter had obeyed. Feeling a terrible sense of foreboding later that day, Rockwell had decided to defy Joseph and go to Carthage anyway, only to be met on the way by another Mormon fleeing back to Nauvoo. This man had been an eyewitness to the murder, and his testimony was unshakable, so Porter, after single-handedly turning back the mob that was chasing the man, had turned his horse and headed back to Nauvoo with the awful news.

"They've killed him . . ." In the distance it sounded more like a sob now.

Who was this man who so keenly felt the death of Joseph Smith—this man who had risked his own life on innumerable occasions while in service to the Church that Joseph Smith had been inspired to restore, that he had been martyred for? Quite simply Rockwell was the Prophet's oldest friend, having known him longer than anyone else in the Church, save members of Joseph Smith's own family. Joseph and Porter had met when Porter was just six years old and Joseph thirteen. There had been no First Vision then—just a young man who was kind to a little boy. Now their mortal friendship had come to an end.

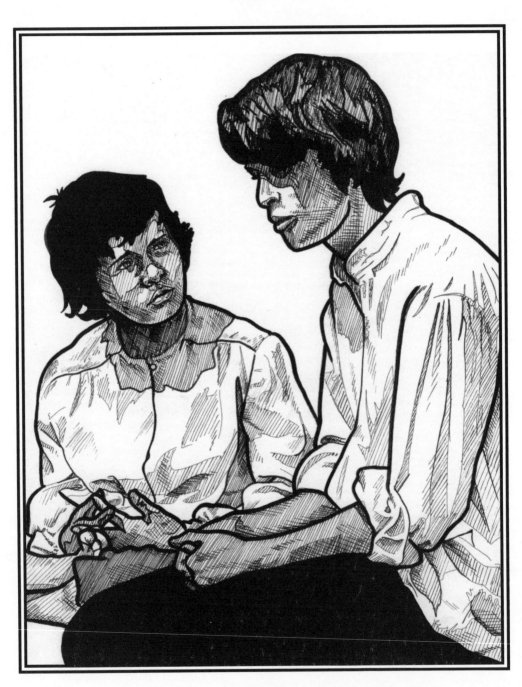

SHARED ADVERSITY

AFTER ENDURING MUCH OF THE "Little Ice Age" that tormented New England in the first decades of the 1800s, as evidenced by snow in June, Orin Rockwell, Porter Rockwell's father, decided to abandon his farm in Massachusetts and move farther into the frontier, then defined as the upstate region of New York State. While his decision was economic, not religious, he and his young family would one day acknowledge that the hand of God had guided them to a farm adjacent to what would soon be Joseph Smith Sr.'s farm, two years later after relocating from Sharon, Vermont.

After the Smiths moved to Palmyra in 1819, their family and the Rockwells soon became close friends and spent many evenings together when the work of the day was done.

Although just six years old, the Rockwells' oldest son Orrin Porter Rockwell was drawn immediately to Joseph Smith and managed to become his friend. Joseph treated him like a younger brother, and Porter idolized Joseph. In later years he spoke of how much he loved being with the Smith family when work and time permitted.

The bond between them would deepen into a lifelong friendship when the younger boy accidentally broke his leg. Injuries were not uncommon on the frontier, and there was nothing out of the ordinary with a broken leg. Unfortunately for Porter, the doctor who was called in to set the leg erred in the way he handled the procedure, and when the bones mended, Porter's broken leg was nearly two inches shorter than the uninjured leg. This gave him a lifelong limp that was a source of embarrassment and distress.

While most of the boys in the area used his disability as a reason to taunt and torment young Porter, Joseph Smith had a very different view of the disability because he too had a limp—the result of surgery on his leg. Joseph's limp was particularly evident when the weather was bad and cold.

Having a similar handicap, the two boys developed a strong bond of friendship that would last to the very last day of Joseph's life. One can imagine the scene of two boys walking down some dusty lane in the countryside comparing who had the best limp.

Joseph Smith's friendship with Porter may also lead to an ambiguous entry in Joseph Smith's personal history referring to activities in his youth that were unbecoming but that he never fully explained to most. It's possible that at least one of these unbecoming activities was Joseph Smith's defending young Porter Rockwell if he ever came upon a group of boys taunting and teasing the young boy. Joseph was not afraid to use his fists if the situation called for it.

In time the tables would be turned, allowing Porter Rockwell to become the bodyguard to the much-harassed Joseph Smith. Porter gave as well as he got, often putting his own life in danger to protect his childhood friend. He almost certainly would have changed the outcome of events at Carthage Jail had Joseph Smith not specifically ordered him to return to Nauvoo on the day of the assassination. Otherwise, Porter, by then a skilled marksman, would not have stood idly by while the mob carried out its insidious work. That was the one occasion when Porter was not meant to be at Joseph's side, and it left Porter bereft for the rest of his life.

Still, their shared adversity brought Joseph and Porter together as brothers. Joseph Smith wrote an entry in his diary saying that Porter was a loyal friend, and "my heart dearly loves him."

Can't I Stay Up and
Keep the Pine Torch Lit?

BEFORE THE SPRING OF 1820, it isn't known if the Smith and Rockwell families broached the subject of religion. It is likely that they did, but to what extent? It was an era of no small religious excitement in the villages of Palmyra and Manchester. The religious affiliation of the Rockwells is not known, but the record of the Smith family is much clearer, being divided over which denominations to align themselves with.

Everything changed in a grove of trees "on the morning of a beautiful, clear day" in 1820. After the First Vision, in which Joseph Smith was first overwhelmed by the force of Satan and then was delivered by a shaft of light, "above the brightness of the sun," in which he beheld the Father and the Son, it was clear that he was to join none of the religions in the area but to wait for a greater work reserved for him.

After that, the two families' visits together took on a very different character, with earnest discussions of visions, angelic visitations, and spiritual manifestations. These topics were openly talked about by the Smiths and Rockwells, with young Joseph at the center of the discussions. How soon after the First Vision the Prophet Joseph Smith spoke of the experience with the Rockwells is speculative. He had learned to be careful with whom he talked concerning the vision. After the fall of 1823, with the visit of the angel Moroni, Joseph was more open to tell the Rockwells of his experiences during their evening visits.

During one such visit at the Rockwell home, the evening grew late, and Mother Rockwell ordered her children to bed. Porter was ten years old and the oldest of the children. He protested being sent off and begged to stay up just awhile longer to "keep the pine torch lit." The pine torch was the source of light for their home and was needed to keep the house illuminated so the adults could listen to Joseph.

Joseph's stories of angels and golden plates surely filled Porter's young mind with thoughts of adventure and the reality of God and his desire to restore the gospel to the earth. Porter was a true believer and would one day be among the first to join the Church. He would also be one of the few who never questioned or abandoned Joseph Smith, as so many of the early Saints did. But Porter's faith was unshakable—he had heard the story of the Restoration as it happened and directly from the mouth of the Prophet of this dispensation.

TREASURE HUNTING

Joseph Smith was often criticized for his experience as a treasure seeker. Today people go out with metal detectors to find old coins and war memorabilia. In Joseph's time it was a commonly held theory that there were ancient buried treasures left from the colonial and exploration periods. Joseph was indeed employed by a farmer who paid him to go treasure hunting with him, often at night. Few things were secret in such a small village like Palmyra, so people were aware of his activities. Joseph's story of finding gold plates buried in a hill played into this, and for some people the very serious revelations of the restored gospel were intermingled with tales of a treasure seeker who preferred to dig idly for buried gold than to give an honest day's work. This reflected negatively on his character. Others were jealous of his apparent success and were determined to steal the gold that Joseph claimed to have discovered.

Brigham Young said regarding treasure seeking,

> Orrin P. Rockwell is an eyewitness to some powers of removing the treasures of the earth. He was with certain parties that lived nearby where the plates were found that contain the records of the Book of Mormon. There were a great many treasures hid up by the Nephites. Porter was with them one night where there were treasures and they could find them easily enough, but could not obtain them.[3]

---

3 Quoted in *The Complete Discourses of Brigham Young,* edited by Richard S. Van Wagoner (Salt Lake City: Signature Books, 2009), 3136–37.

Brigham Young does not expound on why the various treasure seekers could not extract the Nephite treasures, although it's easy to believe that they were protected, just as were the plates. But it appears from the next story that on other occasions they were successful in extracting treasure—perhaps of a more recent origin.

> I will tell you a story which will be marvelous to most of you. It was told to me by Porter, whom I would believe just as quickly as any man that lives. When he tells a thing he understands he will tell it just as he knows it; he is a man that does not lie. He said that on this particular night, when they were engaged hunting for this old treasure, they dug around the end of a chest for some twenty inches. The chest was about three feet square. One man, who was determined to have the contents of that chest, took his pick and struck into the lid of it, and split through into the chest. The blow took off a piece of the lid, which a certain lady kept in her possession until she died. That chest of money went to the bank. Porter describes it so; he says this is just as true as the heavens are. I have heard others tell the same story. I relate this because it is marvelous to you. But to those who understand these things, it is not marvelous.[4]

Although Porter was fond of telling others of his treasure hunting experiences with Joseph Smith, we have no surviving records that speak directly to any specific story other than this oblique reference by Brigham Young.

---

4 Ibid.

PORTER'S FERRY—
THE TURNING POINT

As THE CHURCH GREW IN strength and numbers, Joseph received a revelation to relocate to Kirtland, Ohio. Most members of the Rockwell family had joined the Church immediately after its organization in 1830, although for unknown reasons Porter's father, Orin, chose not to join until nearly two years later.

When the call came for the Saints to go to Kirtland in 1831, the Rockwells agreed, selling their farm and then traveling by barge on the Erie Canal and then by boat to Fairport, Ohio. Of course, this was a great adventure for young Porter, now over seventeen years old, and as quick as the boat landed, he and some of the other boys jumped ship, waving good-bye to their families. Porter called out that he was going to go visit an uncle living somewhere on the frontier. Porter's mother pleaded with Lucy Mack Smith, the leader of this particular group of pilgrims, saying, "Mother Smith, do get Porter back for he won't mind anybody but you. I told him that if he went we should leave him onshore, but he did as he liked."[5] The other boys quickly returned, but Porter did not. It isn't known whether he ever found his uncle. This story shows both his devotion to the Smith family and his independent streak. He was able to take care of himself even at seventeen years old.

The Rockwells' stay in Kirtland was short-lived because the Prophet Joseph Smith asked them to join a small group of Saints who were to journey farther west to the Big Blue area of

5 Lucy Mack Smith. *Biographical Sketches of Joseph Smith, the Prophet, and His Progenitors for Many Generations."* (Liverpool: S. W. Richards, 1853) 179.

Independence, Missouri, in order to establish a second gathering place for the Church. The Rockwells were with the first group of Mormons to settle there.

Having rejoined the family, Porter set about to help them get things organized on their new farm in Missouri. But there was also spare time to spend with Luana Beebe, the attractive daughter of Isaac and Olive Beebe, another Mormon family sent to settle in Independence. Wanting to find his own way in the world, Porter acquired land in his own name while helping his parents establish their farm.

Luana's parents saw Porter as a capable young man who had the capacity to take care of their daughter. There's also an indication that the Rockwells' close friendship with the Smiths and Porter's close friendship with the Prophet Joseph were also important influences on their consent to let their daughter marry Porter. Luana and Porter were married on February 2, 1832. Their marriage was the first Mormon wedding in Jackson County. Most of the Mormon settlers attended the ceremony and joined in the festivities afterward.

As a responsible and enterprising young man, Porter pondered over how he could earn an income that would take care of his new family. Because of the constant stream of Mormon and other settlers moving into Missouri, Porter was struck with the idea of building a ferryboat to cross the Big Blue River near Independence. His father liked the idea and agreed to help him with this new enterprise. It was an immediate success, as so many of Porter's business ventures would be in the coming years. But he learned a hard lesson—he failed to obtain a business license. In February 1833, he was charged with a misdemeanor for operating a ferry without a license. He quickly resolved the issue, and charges were dropped.

In time, Porter built a home near the ferry which, because of its favorable location, was often used as a site for religious meetings of the Saints. One day of particular significance was April 6, 1833—the third anniversary of the founding of the Church in Palmyra. The Jackson County Saints held a conference to commemorate the occasion at what was now known as Porter's Ferry.

The future looked bright for the young Rockwell couple, with a successful business and nice home. Unfortunately it was a false sense of security, as mobster persecution would rear its ugly head to end their tranquility. On July 20, 1833, while Porter and his father were working at the ferry, an armed mob approached them. The members of the mob were white but had disguised themselves as Indians. As the mob approached the Rockwell men, they forced them to take them across to the Mormon side of the river, while taunting them with threats of what they would do to the Mormon women, children, and farms. The two Rockwells were not armed, and so they were helpless to stop them. No one knows what Porter thought, but the next time the mobs attacked, he made a decision that would change his life and the history of the Church.

This change in Porter happened during a series of raids in early November 1833. On one occasion, Porter's parents' home was attacked. At the first signal that evil was approaching, Sarah Rockwell sent her husband and young sons to the nearby woods to hide, knowing that the mob would beat or kill them if they found them. That the men were not there enraged the mob, and they did their worst to the Rockwell property, destroying everything in the home while holding Porter's terrified mother and two of her young daughters at knifepoint. During all of this the men in the mob kept demanding to know where Sarah's husband was, where the boys were, and why they weren't there. Her only response was that he was not home. The mob was angry as their bloodlust went unquenched.

But as bad as it was for Sarah Rockwell, it was just as agonizing for Orin Rockwell to look on from his hiding place, doing his best to calm the fears of his young boys while his mind raced to the unimaginable fears of what could happen to his wife and daughters. When the mob finally had their way with the Rockwell property, they vanished into the night. Fortunately, the women were unharmed, and Orin and the boys made their way back to what was left of their home. It was an agonizing situation for the Saints to endure—not only from the fear of what could happen to them, but from the sense of injustice they felt, knowing that they were law-abiding citizens of the United States who were left defenseless by the state and federal government against these unlawful marauders. Unfortunately, similar scenes were played out at many Mormon farms up and down the river.

One of the defining moments in Porter's life occurred when his own family was attacked while he was working at the ferry. The mob attacked his house with an insane fury, first tearing the roof off the house by attaching ropes to the roof and then to their horses, pulling until the timbers were torn apart. The mob then went to work pulling down every log from the walls of the small cabin that had been Porter and Luana's home. When Porter returned home, he was stunned by what he saw: his young bride standing by the remains of their home, sobbing in fear. He comforted her as best he could, with promises of rebuilding their home. But Porter's young mind also probably obsessed on the injustice of what had happened—not just to him, but to his parents and to all the other Saints who had been the victims of such mindless outrage. From that day forward, Porter never went unarmed.

In order to better protect his family and the Saints, Rockwell started taking regular shooting practice in the woods. With a rifle you need to learn to take careful aim and to bring your target clearly and steadily into the gun sights. With a pistol you need to keep it loose and accessible, drawing and pointing to shoot rather than aiming, in Porter's case drawing from pockets or his belt since he never wore a holster. Porter was superb at both approaches, as was noted by Saints and leaders of the Church. He soon became a force to be reckoned with.

Every decision has a price. In Porter's case, the decision to defend himself, his family, the Prophet, and other Church leaders meant that he would eventually become a gunman. As noted earlier, he was never found guilty of anything but self-defense or acting lawfully in his role as a member of the militia or as a deputy marshal. But his experience in Jackson County hardened him.

For example, many years later Porter was leading a group of men whose horses had been stolen by a group of Indians. In the 1800s, horse theft was considered a capital offense. As Porter and his group closed in on the Indians, he was able to retrieve the stolen horses. Porter demanded to know who among the group of Indians was guilty of the crime, but the Indians refused to answer. So Porter selected three at random, gave the group another chance to let the culprits step forward, and then ordered the three shot as justice for the robbery. The fact that the Indian group and those in Porter's own party thought this was an acceptable action on his part shows just how different nineteenth-century America was compared to today. To provide accurate context, it's important to consider a couple of points. Firstly, in the wilderness a man's horse was often his only way to find safety. Without it, he could easily die. Secondly, in spite of the legality of this frontier justice, the fact that Porter could do such a thing shows that he had become a different man than he was when he and his father were helpless to resist the marauders of Jackson County demanding a ferry transport.

A Trail of Sorrow—
Jackson, Clay, and Caldwell

IN SPITE OF PORTER'S PROMISE to himself that he would not be driven out of Jackson County, he was. Almost since their arrival in Missouri, the Mormons had endured countless beatings, their homes being destroyed by mobs, and their crops being burned. Some men, including Bishop Edward Partridge, had been kidnapped, tarred, and feathered. There had even been a number of the Saints who were murdered. Women had also been attacked and molested.[6]

On a very personal level, Porter's brother-in-law, George Beebe, was beaten senseless by a mob. This was in addition to the terror his wife, mother, and sisters had endured.

The Saints tried to fight back, but they were far outnumbered and certainly outgunned. Eventually they capitulated and signed a pledge that they would leave Jackson County by January 1, 1834. Once this agreement was in place, the Mormons sought help from Missouri Governor Daniel Dunklin, pleading first for help in invalidating the pledge, as there was nothing in state or federal law that made forcing contracts with intimidation a legal practice. Secondly, if the government couldn't protect them in that fashion, they sought assurance that they would have help in an orderly and safe withdrawal. There were also questions about how dispose of their property at a fair value; how to provide food for their families in the middle of winter; how to pass safely through those parts of Missouri held by hostile neighbors, and so forth. Many of the Mormons had invested their life savings in their homes and farms and couldn't just walk away with nothing. They needed

---

6 *History of the Church* 1:415.

assurances that they could sue the perpetrators for damages and loss of property, for "abuse, for defamation as to ourselves" and "if advisable to try the mobbers for treason against the government."7

Governor Dunklin flatly refused any assistance, advising the Mormons to take their grievances to the courts. With a growing sense of hopelessness for their situation, they retained legal counsel from a law firm that included Alexander Doniphan, a courageous non-Mormon lawyer who was also an officer in the state militia and in the state legislature. Doniphan would eventually play a crucial role in the survival of the Church. But at this point the courts offered little protection. Even when a court rendered judgment in behalf of a particular member of the Church, or the Church itself, it was almost impossible to collect damages since it's up to the executive branch of government to direct the state militia—something Governor Dunklin had already refused to do.

Eventually, the Saints resigned themselves to the fact that they would have to meet the deadline and leave Jackson County for Clay County. Among the Mormons who crossed the Missouri River in that bleak winter of 1834 were the Rockwells—Porter and his little family, as well as his parents, brothers, and sisters. They lost everything but what they could carry. Emily M. Austin, sister-in-law of Newel Knight, wrote of the hardships they endured on this particular exodus.

> The Colesville Church, together with 20 or 30 other branches of the Mormon Church, had already arrived on the northern side of the river and more were on their way. We lived in tents until winter set in, and did our cooking in the wind and the storms. Log heaps were our parlor stoves, the cold, wet ground our velvet carpets, and the crying of little children our piano . . . while the shivering sick people hovered

7 Ibid.

over burning log piles here and there, some begging for cold water, others for hot coffee or tea.[8]

Although the Saints rallied in Clay County and built new dwellings and started to establish farms to support their families, their stay there was short. In less than three years the good citizens of Clay County insisted that their Mormon neighbors leave. Though not as violent as in Jackson County, life was miserable for the struggling branches of the Church, and soon they had to either leave or renounce their religion.

Still, the Saints were not without friends. Alexander Doniphan and others in the state legislature worked to create a new county exclusively for the Mormons to be known as Caldwell County. It would comprise largely uninhabited land at the north end of Ray County, since the established citizens of Ray also made it clear they did not want the Mormons to settle in their county. For a nation that prided itself on being a haven for those seeking religious freedom, this hostility seems inexplicable.

Porter and Luana, along with their two young daughters, Emily and Caroline, made their way to the small community of Far West, the newest Mormon settlement. They had gone as far as civilization extended in an attempt to stay out of the way of their non-Mormon neighbors. Porter's parents and younger siblings were with them. As they rolled up their sleeves and got to work building yet again, it was clear that Porter's faith in the Church had not wavered. But it seems fair to speculate that his faith in government had.

---

8 Emily M. Austin. *Life Among the Mormons.* (Madison, Wisconsin: M. J. Cantwell, 1882) 72–73.

PORTER AND THE DANITES

THE ROCKWELLS HAD BEEN LIVING in Far West for more than a year when Joseph Smith arrived in the spring of 1831. The Prophet needed a fresh start after his financial problems in Ohio, including the failure of the Kirtland Safety Society and the apostasy of some leaders of the Church. He arrived to find that Far West had grown into a thriving village of 5,000—quite sizeable by frontier standards. The town boasted of hundreds of buildings, 2,000 farms, a public square, and a temple site.[9] With large numbers of Saints arriving weekly, the town was bursting at the seams, and pressure was growing to settle new members outside the boundaries of Caldwell County.

The old settlers who were not members of the Church resisted expansion, and conflict occurred over the same issues that the Mormons had faced in Jackson County: growing political power, religious differences, and the more friendly view the Mormons had of the Native Americans, to name a few. But the biggest pressure point was slavery: the Missourians supported it while Mormons generally opposed it. While this problem was not unique to Mormons and non-Mormons, it added to the passions on both sides.

Joseph Smith's more immediate problem was dissension in the Church. Some of his most vocal detractors had followed him to Far West from Kirtland, hoping to extract revenge for the losses they'd suffered financially, including John Whitmer, W. W. Phelps, and Oliver Cowdery, who were soon excommunicated from the Church. Their expulsion followed proper protocol,

9 Richard L. Bushman. *Joseph Smith: Rough Stone Rolling.* (New York: Knopf, 2005) 342–43.

and each of the detractors had a chance to tell their story to the high council. But the members in Far West had endured enough sorrow and persecution for their beliefs that they were not open to the claims of traitors; they wanted them out of Far West. Though Joseph Smith's usual pattern in dealing with internal Church problems was to reprimand, reconcile, forgive, and then welcome back individuals, Sidney Rigdon, then a member of the presidency, was not so accommodating. He authored an ultimatum demanding that the dissenters leave the county immediately. Porter Rockwell and Hyrum Smith were among the eighty-three signers of this document. Porter's X was the sixty-ninth signature.[10] Each man had his reason for signing, but Porter did it for loyalty to his friend Joseph Smith. After all that the Rockwells had endured for the Church, it was a matter of integrity to stand by Joseph at this time. Later, during the Nauvoo period of the Church, Joseph would ask Porter to be his personal bodyguard—a request to which Porter quickly agreed. "Your enemies are my enemies," he said at that time. That's likely how he felt during the controversy in Far West.

It may also explain why Porter did something in Far West that was for him quite uncharacteristic. He joined a secret militant group of defenders of the Church, the Sons of Dan, or Danites. His brief membership in this society troubled him for the rest of his life. In fact, his falsely attributed role as a leader of the Danite militia, and the alleged acts they were accused of through the years, was one of the main charges leveled at him by the *Salt Lake Tribune* following his death.

Dr. Sampson Avard was a convert to the Mormon faith when he arrived in Far West. He saw firsthand the mounting fears of the Saints caused by enemies from within the Church who were now in collusion with enemy mobs. Avard saw the opportunity to promote himself into a position of leadership within the community. Playing on their fears, Avard approached a number

---

10 Schindler, 1st ed., 39.

of prominent men in Far West to see who would be willing to join a secret militia that would band together for self-defense. This was not uncommon in early American history. What made Avard's society unique is that he insisted on ritual practice, such as oath taking, in addition to military organization and discipline. These Danite rituals included vows with religious overtones, passwords, and signals. Eventually he organized preparatory meetings with small numbers in attendance, urging people to keep the meetings secret so that enemies of the Church could not organize against the Danites.

The first full-scale meeting was held in June 1838, which many men attended, including Porter Rockwell. Avard explained that the purpose of the militia was to defend the Church from traitors from within its own ranks. In view of the high-profile excommunications that had recently taken place in Far West, suspicion was high, and Avard's proposal was met with a degree of enthusiasm. By the end of the meeting, however, Avard unintentionally revealed the real reason he wanted to organize the group: to use the Danites for personal gain by plundering and pillaging the enemies of the Saints as they were driven out of town. Sampson Avard reserved the power for himself to determine who was and was not an enemy. Several of the men in attendance at the meeting immediately denounced Avard, emphatically asserting that his purposes were against Church principles and, in fact, criminal.[11]

Avard rebuffed their challenge, claiming that there was no justice in man's laws, as evidenced by the fierce persecution endured by the Saints with no protection from the state or federal government. He asserted the only laws worth obeying were God's laws. This added to the confusion of the evening, with some being in favor of Avard's proposal while some prominent men still opposed him. For example, Lorenzo Dow Young denounced him and went directly to Brigham Young to

11 Schindler, 1st ed., 48.

report what was taking place and then to Joseph Smith, who, Lorenzo Young said, "has suspicions that some secret wickedness was being carried out by Dr. Avard."[12] Upon learning of Avard's sedition, Church authorities cited him, and he was cut out of the Danites for his wickedness. Joseph eventually denounced Avard for what he was, saying of him, "Satan himself was no less busy in striving to stir up mischief in the camp of the Saints, and among the most conspicuous of his willing devotees was one Dr. Sampson Avard."[13]

In spite of Avard's withdrawal, the Danites continued for a time. Members of the Danites even sat on the reviewing stand for the Independence Day Celebration on July 4, 1838. In view of the hostilities leveled against the Saints, it was not unreasonable to have groups committed to their self-defense. But the Danites in practice were not the insidious organization that Avard had advocated, even though Church critics have made damning allegations against them ever since. Sampson Avard remained somewhat loyal to the Mormons for a time and even acted as a surgeon for the Mormons during the impending Missouri War, but at the end of the conflict he turned traitor and testified against Joseph Smith. Avard went free during the time that Joseph and other Church leaders spent five months in Liberty Jail.

Many have accused Joseph Smith of starting the Danites, using Sampson Avard as a cover. Because Porter was Joseph's friend and bodyguard, it is often assumed that Rockwell committed crimes under the cloak of Danite protection. But it makes no sense that these allegations are true. If Joseph relied on the Danites, why would he publicly denounce Avard and the operations of his militia, up to the point of excommunicating him?

Porter was among the first to join the Danites in Far West. However, contrary to anti-Mormon myth, he was a minor player compared to the far more prominent men on its rolls.

---

12 James A. Little. "Biography of Lorenzo Dow Young." (Utah Historical Quarterly, 1946), 51–53.
13 *History of the Church* 13:178–80.

A careful look at history shows that the Danite militia merged with the larger and better-organized Mormon militia during the Missouri War. Since the Danite organization was short-lived, Porter did not advance into its leadership ranks. Harold Schindler, one of Porter's biographers, drew the following conclusion after an exhaustive study of Rockwell's life:

> Of all who joined the order, no one suffered the notoriety of membership more than did Orrin Porter Rockwell. Indeed, he went to his grave branded with the inglorious title of Danite chieftain, an unworthy and unfounded appellation.[14]

14 Schindler, 1st ed., 43–44.

THE MISSOURI WAR

A S THE ATTACKS OF THE anti-Mormon vigilantes grew in intensity, the Saints defended themselves. They had tried a different approach in Jackson County, and it had failed miserably. Now there was shooting on both sides. As the Mormon militia flexed its muscles, the Missourians petitioned their new governor, Lilburn W. Boggs, for help in driving the Mormons out. While serving as lieutenant governor in the previous administration, Boggs had been vehemently anti-Mormon, in part because the Mormons had purchased some land in Jackson County that he had wanted to buy. He was also distrustful of their growing numbers, which inevitably provided political power. And like most Missourians, he supported slavery. From his twisted point of view, the Mormons were a problem. Now that he was the governor, he called out the state militia. The Saints came into violent conflict with the enemy militia, culminating in the Battle of Crooked River in which four men lost their lives. The battle was prompted by unfounded rumors spread in Ray and Clay Counties by Mormon dissenters, including David and John Whitmer, Oliver Cowdery, and William Phelps. On the Mormon side, rumors were spread that the Ray militia was armed and moving toward the Mormons. The battle ended with both sides withdrawing, but the results were horrendous for the Mormons because of Governor Boggs's subsequently issued extermination order. Boggs asserted that the extermination order was necessary because the Mormons were in open rebellion against the state.

While Porter's exact role in the battle is not known, many stories were told about him. As one story goes, Porter fought like a devil, constantly exposing himself to enemy fire. When the battle ended, Porter examined his coat and clothing, finding them riddled with bullet holes, but he was unharmed.

The Mormons were eventually forced to surrender their weapons to the Missouri militia. Alexander Doniphan, a brigadier general in the Missouri militia and former attorney for the Mormons, accepted the surrender of Joseph and other Church leaders. General Lucas ordered Doniphan to execute the prisoners. To his credit, Doniphan defied his superior, telling him that executing the prisoners was cold-blooded murder. He further told the general that if the prisoners were executed, he, Doniphan, would personally hold the general responsible even if he had to do so before the highest court in the state. General Lucas backed down. This is one of the rare times in history when a military officer defied a direct order from a superior officer on moral grounds and succeeded in preventing a crime from taking place.

The only documented account of Porter's involvement in the war was during the siege of Far West by General Lucas's troops. The record shows that Porter was assigned to the breastworks at the outer defenses of the city. In such a position he would have been witness to the surrender and arrest of his friend Joseph Smith, who was then to be taken to the confinement of Liberty Jail.

ATTEMPTED ESCAPE FROM LIBERTY JAIL

WITH THE SAINTS' CAPITULATION IN the Mormon War, they were forced to flee for their lives yet again. Land was discovered in a swamp on the Illinois bank of the Mississippi River, and a new exodus was begun to a site that Joseph Smith renamed Nauvoo, Hebrew for "beautiful place." The only advantage this land held for the beleaguered Saints was that it was free of Missourians. But in time Joseph's name for the site would become a prophecy fulfilled when the Mormons turned it into one of the most prosperous and thriving cities on the Western frontier.

While Joseph was in Liberty Jail, a number of men in Far West signed a written covenant with the Missourians that pledged the signers to sell their properties to help the poor and destitute among the Mormons to leave Missouri. These members of the Church were to stay behind as their fellow members struggled back across Missouri and up the Mississippi River to the shallows of Nauvoo. The signers would stay behind to see that affairs were settled with the victorious Missourians. Porter Rockwell was among the men who left their mark on the document.[15] Having worked to build up a small measure of temporal security, he now sacrificed all of it to help keep the Saints together.

Rockwell's family had to leave Far West as soon as possible. Because Porter was committed to staying behind, it's likely that his wife and children went in company with Porter's father during their exodus.

---

15 *History of the Church* 3:251–54.

During this period Porter received the priesthood at a Church conference in Far West, being ordained a deacon in the Aaronic priesthood at twenty-five years old. It would not be until the Nauvoo era that he would advance into the higher Melchizedek priesthood when he was ordained a Seventy, a position he held until his death in 1878.[16]

With his family on their way to Nauvoo, Porter became a messenger for the Prophet Joseph Smith from his jail cell in Liberty, most often carrying communications to Brigham Young. To some degree the Prophet was able to manage the affairs of the Church and to stay informed about the success of the exodus through these messages. When Porter visited the prisoners, he would bring them food and drink.[17]

During one of Porter's visits, the Prophet Joseph asked him to help the prisoners escape. They had already tried an escape by bolting through their open cell door during someone's visit, but the jailer and guard had successfully slammed the door in their faces. In what had to be a minor miracle, or a sleight of hand, Porter was able to smuggle in two augers for the prisoners to use in boring a hole through the wall of the prison. With nothing but time on their hands, the prisoners went to work on the project with zeal. But it was a big job since the walls of Liberty Jail were four feet thick. Still, they made good progress and finally bored their way through the wood and stone right up to the point that they were ready to dislodge the last stone between them and freedom. Unfortunately, their work had taken a toll on the augers, which gave out and broke. So close to escaping, victory eluded them nonetheless.

The next time Porter came to see them, Joseph asked him to bring replacement handles. Unfortunately this time Porter was caught by the jailer as he tried to smuggle the long wooden handles in. Joseph Smith would later write in an account of the event:

16 For reference, see *Improvement Era*, vol. 5, February 1901, 309.
17 *History of the Church* 3:257.

Unfortunately, for us, the timber of the wall being very hard, our auger handles gave out and hindered us longer than we expected. We applied to a friend, but a very slight incautious act on his part gave rise to some suspicions, and before we could fully succeed our plan was discovered. We had everything in readiness but the last stone, and we could have made our escape in one minute, and should have succeeded admirably, had it not been for a little imprudence, or over-anxiety on the part of our friend.[18]

Joseph went on to say that the sheriff and jailer didn't blame them for trying to escape, but Joseph referred to the hole they had made in the wall as "a fine breach that cost the county a round sum."[19]

The dark days that Joseph and his brethren spent in Liberty Jail are well documented. Eventually their imprisonment became an embarrassment to Governor Boggs and the state of Missouri. Many historians now believe that the transportation of the prisoners to another jail was orchestrated by the governor himself so that Joseph and the others could escape. Extremely negative reports in the national press about the vigilante persecution of the Mormons and Boggs's extermination order had possibly pushed the governor to be rid of the Mormon issue altogether.

Joseph and the prisoners were transferred to the custody of Sheriff William Morgan and his deputies on April 15, 1839. The prisoners were all placed in a two-horse-drawn wagon. The exact details of what happened next are murky. The sheriff and his deputies got drunk, allowing the prisoners to escape on two horses they had purchased. A likely account of what happened is that when entering Boone County, the party stopped one evening at the home of a local farmer who was also the local

18 *History of the Church* 3:292.
19 Ibid.

judge. Joseph's brother Hyrum was told by the sheriff to go into the nearest town and purchase jugs of whiskey for the sheriff and the deputies. That evening the sheriff and his deputies downed the contents of the jugs. Everyone in the party—deputies, prisoners, and sheriff—spent the night on the judge's parlor floor. During the night one of the deputies woke Hyrum up, took him to the barn, and told him to saddle two horses and make his escape with the other prisoners. Hyrum didn't need a second invitation and so quickly made his way back to the house where he awakened Joseph and the other prisoners. In short order they went out to the barn and made their escape.[20]

Again, the facts are not known. We do know that on April 22, 1839, Joseph, Hyrum, and the other escaped prisoners rode into Quincy, Illinois, where they were free men. Joseph was welcomed by family and friends, including Porter Rockwell.

If the sheriff was ordered by the governor to let the prisoners escape, he paid a price for it. On his return to Gallatin, he was surrounded and attacked by his fellow citizens for letting "Joe Smith" get out of his grasp, and the sheriff was run out of town for his "incompetence."[21]

We've offered two possible explanations for the escape—incompetence by drunk deputies or direct orders by powerful, embarrassed men. There may have been another reason for the escape. Several weeks after the escape, Sheriff Morgan turned up in Quincy, where he was seen talking with Joseph Smith. People speculated that Joseph was paying for the horses that he had used in the escape, or, as some have suggested, he was paying an $800 bribe for allowing the prisoners to escape. If it was a bribe, it was an expensive one, since $800 was a princely amount in 1838—but certainly worth the price to have these men set free before a mock trial could be convened. No one knows for sure, but it was an interesting ending to the troubled Liberty Jail incarceration.

---

20 *History of the Church* 3:320–22.
21 Schindler, 1st ed., 65.

The Rockwells had the chance to live close to the Prophet once more, which pleased Porter. But the years of relocating and constant harassment of the mobs and anti-Mormons took a fatal toll on Porter's father, Orin, who died on September 22, 1839. The unhealthy conditions that the Saints endured in Illinois when they first arrived, following the physical difficulties of the exodus from Missouri, almost certainly were responsible for Orin Rockwell's death.

Still, the Saints had finally found a resting place with room to grow. Since no one else wanted Nauvoo, they had the chance to turn it into a city of their own liking. Eventually Porter would build a new home for his family in Nauvoo on the corner of Munson and Partridge Streets, directly across from the home of Heber C. Kimball. The future looked brighter than it had for years.

PORTER AND JOSEPH
IN WASHINGTON DC

THE SAINTS NEEDED MONEY. MORE than that they needed reassurance that they were still citizens of the United States in good standing. Joseph Smith had received inspiration that the Constitution was inspired and was proud to call himself an American, yet little of America's tolerance for religion and political affiliation had been extended to the Mormons. So he decided to lead a delegation to Washington DC to seek relief and redress.

On October 29, 1834, Joseph Smith, Sidney Rigdon, Elias Higbee, and Orrin Porter Rockwell kissed their families good-bye as they stepped into a carriage to strike out for the nation's capital. They planned to petition the president and Congress for a redress of their losses at the hands of the Missourians. They couldn't make an appeal where it properly belonged—the statehouse in Missouri—since there was an extermination order out against them.

Joseph needed someone with Porter's abilities and loyalty to serve as a bodyguard, a role which Porter readily accepted. By the time the men reached Columbus, Ohio, Sidney Rigdon had fallen ill. After a short deliberation Joseph decided to leave Sidney in the care of a local doctor, protected by Porter, while Joseph and Elias Higbee continued to the capital.

By the time Porter and Sidney Rigdon arrived in Washington DC, Joseph had already made important contacts on Capitol Hill. Joseph asked Porter to add his own affidavit, and a proxy for his deceased father, to be added to the many others that were being presented to Congress. Porter dictated a list of the property that the Rockwells had lost to the Missourians and found that the amount was the extremely large sum of $5,000.[22] Porter's affidavit to Congress was dated February 3, 1840.

Unfortunately, the Senate Judiciary Committee decided against the Mormons' claims and returned all of the affidavits to the Mormon delegation. Higbee then submitted the claims to the House of Representatives, again to no avail.[23]

Joseph's meeting with President Martin Van Buren had a similar result, although the president's response was more empathetic, if no more meaningful, when he said, "Gentlemen, your cause is just, but I can do nothing for you." President Van Buren was afraid he would lose the Missouri vote if he helped the Mormons.

Once again, Porter Rockwell was a witness to history. On the return to Illinois, Porter said good-bye to Joseph and the others so he could visit his sister in Handen, Ohio. He finally arrived home in Nauvoo to his wife and children in early March 1839, after nearly five months' absence. He was delighted to hold his five-month-old son, Orrin DeWitt Rockwell, who had been born only two days before Porter had left for Washington DC.

---

22 One ounce of gold sold for $20.65 in 1838. Gold sold for $945.00 in 2009—a multiple of nearly 50 times.

23 *History of the Church* 4:80–81.

ATTEMPTED ASSASSINATION OF GOVERNOR BOGGS

PORTER HAD COMFORTABLY SETTLED LUANA and their three children in Nauvoo, and they were expecting their fourth child. But there were tensions in the marriage. The Rockwells' life on the frontier had been hard, with Porter often absent as he worked to support his family and to serve the needs of Church leaders. Perhaps it was too much for Luana to bear. At any rate, as the birth of their fourth child approached, she made a difficult demand on Porter: she wanted to go back to Independence, Missouri, to be with her uncle Calvin Bebee and his wife so they could help her with the birth. Porter was a wanted man in Missouri for his role in the Missouri War, and the Missourians were particularly keen to get Porter since he was such a close friend of Joseph Smith. It would have been far safer for Luana to stay in Nauvoo, where there were a number of competent midwives and where she would not have to endure the burden of a journey at the advanced stages of her pregnancy. Still, she insisted and Porter complied.

In February 1842, Porter and his eight-months pregnant wife left Nauvoo for Independence. There is no record of whether they took their three children with them or if they left them in the care of Porter's mother, Sarah Rockwell. Porter never said why he agreed to Luana's wishes.

When the couple finally arrived at Calvin Bebee's home in Independence, Porter saw to his wife's needs and comfort. Knowing of the danger he faced in Independence if anyone recognized him, Porter adopted an alias, calling himself James B. Brown. To earn money he got a job training horses for a local farmer and caring for the farmer's prized stallion, a job to which he was superbly suited.

Their fourth child, Sarah, was born March 25, 1842. She was named after Porter's mother. Whatever hope Porter nurtured that their marriage would hold together was lost by year's end, however, when Luana decided to leave her children to the care of Porter's mother. Eventually she would return to Nauvoo and divorce Porter. Years later, others would claim that Porter's clandestine journey to Independence had a more sinister motive—to kill the former governor Lilburn Boggs at the order of Joseph Smith.

On the rainy evening of May 6, 1842, Lilburn Boggs was at home. After dinner he settled down to read a newspaper. His two young daughters were in the room with him. His wife and other children were still in the kitchen. Someone outside the home aimed a large pistol at the back of Boggs's head. There was a flash of powder and the crack of a single gunshot as the buckshot smashed through the closed window. Overloaded with powder, the gun went flying from the would-be assassin's hand, who was then seen running from the scene of the crime. Boggs was hit four times from the single shot. Boggs's wife and children ran to his side to find him bleeding from two wounds in his neck and two in the back of his head. William, the eldest son, was sent for help. Sheriff Joseph H. Reynolds arrived with four doctors, one of whom was Boggs's own brother. A large crowd assembled outside the home while the doctors tended to Boggs's wounds. Even in the excitement of the moment, the sheriff began to investigate the scene of the crime. One of the onlookers handed the sheriff a pistol, claiming that he had found it in the mud a few yards from the house. Philip Uhlinger, a local merchant, stepped forward claiming that the pistol was his and that it had been stolen from his store a few days earlier. The gun in question was a large-caliber, German-made pepperbox pistol. Whoever had used the weapon had overcharged it with ball and powder, causing it to fly from his hand when the trigger was pulled. The recovered weapon was the most important piece of evidence collected in the investigation.[24]

Although severely wounded, Boggs would eventually recover, but the mystery of his attempted assassination has never been resolved.

Here's what is known. Uhlinger the merchant, who said the pistol was stolen from his store, at first stated that some slaves had been in his store and must have taken the weapon and either used it in the assassination attempt or sold it to someone who did. He changed his story sometime later and said that the man working for the farmer named Ward (referring to Porter Rockwell) had also been in his store that day and had looked at the pistol. Reynolds began a search for the hired hand named Brown, but he was nowhere to be found. As he learned more about Brown, Reynolds soon concluded that the man he was looking for was none other than the infamous Orrin Porter Rockwell.

Meanwhile, another man, Tompkins, became suspect in the crime. The evidence pointing to this individual was so compelling that a $500 reward was offered in the *Jeffersonian Republic* on May 14, 1842. The newspaper gave a detailed physical description of the man including his approximate age and occupation, a silversmith. The description of the man did not match Rockwell's. The article claimed that the evidence left no doubt of Tompkins's guilt. A week later, however, on May 21, the same newspaper reported that Tompkins was not guilty of the crime and now chose to lay the crime at the feet of Joseph Smith and Orrin Porter Rockwell.

In this revised indictment, the paper claimed that Joseph Smith had prophesied a year earlier that Boggs would die a violent death and that Rockwell was sent to fulfill the prophecy. When Joseph Smith heard of this supposed prophecy, he

24 For reference, see Schindler, 1st ed., 74–75; Lyman L. Palmer. *History of Napa and Lake Counties* (San Francisco, CA: 1881), 106–8; "William M. Boggs, Sketch of Lilburn W. Boggs," *Missouri Historical Review,* vol. 4, January 1910, 106–08.

immediately denied it, and there is no documented evidence that such a prophecy was ever made. Still, a conspiracy by the Mormons to murder their old enemy was picked up by the community and quickly spread throughout Missouri.

Was Porter guilty of the crime? Contemporary evidence supports Rockwell's claim that he was far away from Independence when the Boggs shooting took place. For example, a man fitting the description of Rockwell was seen on a riverboat in St. Louis the day after the shooting took place. If it was Porter, it would have been physically impossible for him to have shot Boggs and made it to St. Louis in that brief period. Second, Porter arrived in Nauvoo about two weeks after the crime took place, which is too short a time for such a long journey.

The most compelling evidence that Rockwell did not shoot Boggs was the weapon itself. Why would Porter steal a gun when he had his own weapons? By stealing a gun he would risk getting caught, foiling his alleged plan to shoot Boggs.

Whoever loaded the pepperbox pistol had overcharged it with powder and ball so that when he touched the trigger, the weapon flew out of his hand. Porter, who was well versed with the use of pistols, knew better than to do that. Besides, he certainly would have had the sense to retrieve the weapon after the shot rather than leave it on the ground as evidence.

Boggs had enemies besides the Mormons, having been a very unpopular governor. His budget for the new statehouse was exorbitant. He also had business rivals, including the shopkeeper Uhlinger, who was a competitor of Boggs's. Why Uhlinger wasn't investigated is a mystery, because the pistol used to shoot Boggs was his. The idea of slaves taking it, or the stranger working for farmer Ward, was too convenient to explain away his own motivations and his ownership of the attempted murder weapon. Still, blaming slaves and Mormons was a pretty safe bet in Missouri at this period, so Uhlinger was successful in avoiding an investigation on his potential role in the sordid affair.

Despite the unmatchable description of the assailant, the conviction with which Tompkins was cited, and the inconsistency in Uhlinger's story, a warrant was issued for Porter's arrest. The day came when Porter was arrested to stand trial for Lilburn Boggs's shooting. After Porter's arrest and imprisonment in Independence, while he awaited trial, a grand jury was convened. After investigating the evidence against Rockwell, they threw the case out for lack of evidence. Consider the political implications—a jury of Missourians failed to bring charges against Porter Rockwell, even though the Mormons were detested in the state. In spite of this acquittal, former governor Boggs maintained throughout his long life that it was Porter who had shot him, and many today still consider him the prime suspect.

When Porter himself was confronted about whether he was the triggerman, he dismissed the accusation by saying, "He's still alive, isn't he?" meaning that if he'd gone after Boggs, the governor would not have survived. When news of the attempted assassination reached Nauvoo, Joseph Smith expressed a similar sentiment when he said, "It couldn't have been Porter—he'd have killed him." Yet 160 years later, Porter is still associated with the shooting of Lilburn Boggs.

Porter on the Lam

THE MISSOURIANS WEREN'T THE ONLY ones to suspect Porter's involvement in the shooting of Lilburn Boggs. By the time Porter arrived in Nauvoo some two weeks after the incident, speculation was circulating throughout the community that he had shot Boggs. John C. Bennett, who had been excommunicated for spiritual wifery (adultery), added fuel to the fire. Bennett had become a vocal opponent of Joseph Smith, and he now started circulating rumors that Joseph had ordered the assassination of Boggs and that Porter had gone to Missouri to accomplish the murder on Joseph's direct orders. Bennett went so far as to have accounts of this nature published in the newspaper.

This created a controversy that dogged Porter wherever he went. Finally, he confronted Bennett directly, telling him, "I don't want my name in your publications. I'm innocent. I'll go anywhere I've ever been because I've never done anything wrong!" To emphasize the point, he reiterated in very clear language, "I have done nothing wrong!" Then he warned Bennett, "Don't use my name again."

Bennett confessed to Porter, "Well, I don't know if you shot Boggs or not—I wasn't there." This confirmed to Porter that Bennett had simply been using him as a way to get even with Joseph Smith, but he was satisfied that Bennett was intimidated enough not to print his name again. It is also a clear declaration by Porter Rockwell himself that he hadn't attempted the assassination.[25]

25 Affidavit of John C. Bennett. "Sworn before Samuel Marshall, Justice of the Peace, Hancock County, Illinois; July 7, 1842; Published in *The Wasp*, July 27, 1842; Bennett. *History of the Saints,* 283; Schindler, 1st ed., 78–79.

Despite Porter's declaration of innocence, officials from Missouri showed up in Nauvoo with an arrest warrant for Joseph Smith and Orrin Porter Rockwell, charging them with conspiracy to commit murder against Lilburn Boggs. The unique grant of power given in the Nauvoo Charter provided a measure of protection to the Prophet. Joseph was able to use a writ of habeas corpus to elude the grasp of Missouri's law long enough to go into hiding. The last thing Joseph needed was to be taken back to Missouri. The Saints in Nauvoo quickly hid Joseph Smith, eluding the authorities.

But Porter wasn't so fortunate, and his attempt to elude these charges was complicated because of his wife's unannounced return from Independence to serve Porter with divorce papers and to turn their children over to the care of Porter's mother, Sarah. After she left, Porter was forced to flee to the East, eventually making his way to Pennsylvania, where he lived for nearly a year. His situation soon became desperate because he couldn't find work. He even went into New Jersey in the hope of finding work there but was unsuccessful because of a severe economic depression gripping the East Coast. One individual struggling to find employment at the time said that the best a man could hope for in those troubled days was to find a job that would give him food for pay and nothing more. Returning to Philadelphia, Porter dictated a letter to Joseph Smith, written by a fellow Latter-day Saint, asking about Joseph's welfare and about his mother and children. After sending the letter, though, Rockwell decided to throw caution to the wind and spend what little money he had left to go down the Ohio River to intersect the Mississippi River so he could make his way back upstream to Illinois.

But this was a mistake. As the steamboat was churning its way up to the dock in St. Louis, a fellow Mormon by the name of Parker recognized Porter and decided to turn him in for the reward. As soon as the boat was tied up, Parker was the first off the boat and ran up to a sheriff near the landing and declared, "Rockwell is on the steamboat—I want the reward money!" The reward was a compelling sum, totaling three thousand dollars, which was far more than a year's wages for most laborers at that time. The reason there was such a bounty on Porter's head is that the Missourians believed that if they could trap Porter, they could lure Joseph Smith back into Missouri.

Porter had no idea that he had been betrayed, so he exited the boat calmly with the rest of the passengers, only to find the sheriff and his deputies waiting for him at the bottom of the ramp. He was quickly arrested, handcuffed, and taken to jail.

While he was in the St. Louis jail for three days, two other individuals claiming to be Mormons called on him and said they were lawyers who would help to defend him. Gaining his confidence, they convinced him that he was likely to have his weapons confiscated, so at their urging he turned over two pistols, a gold watch, and his bowie knife for their safekeeping. Well, that was the last time he saw those two men and his possessions. He'd been swindled on top of all his other problems.

After three days in the jail, he was handcuffed to a deputy, put on a stagecoach, and sent off toward Independence. It was not a pleasant journey. The weather that February was particularly cold and rainy, so they spent the time inside the carriage shivering. At night they stayed in inns along the way, with the deputy sleeping in the warm bed while handcuffed to Porter, who was forced to sleep on the hardwood floor with no blankets.

On one stretch of the journey the stagecoach driver had too much liquor to drink at one of the saloons, and he was driving while drunk, with a bottle in one hand, the reins in the other. Driving the horses too fast for the road, he oversteered on a wet corner, and the stagecoach slid into a tree, breaking the kingpin holding the horses to the coach. Even though handcuffed, Porter volunteered to make the repair, so he got out of the coach, found his way to the boot at the rear of the stagecoach where a spare kingpin was stored, and successfully made the repair. Recognizing the incompetence of the driver, Porter volunteered to drive the coach, but the deputy was afraid that Porter would try to escape, so he refused the offer.

A few miles farther down the road, the driver again took a turn too sharply, this time overturning the coach and tumbling all the passengers inside. With both women and men in the carriage, it was an embarrassing mess as the rattled passengers finally crawled out of the coach into the miserable night. The men tipped the coach upright, and this time the passengers insisted that Porter drive the coach. Porter calmed the frightened horses, carefully checked the coach to make sure it was roadworthy, climbed up onto the seat with the deputy next to him, and then proceeded to drive himself to jail.

Upon arriving in Independence, Porter was turned over to the local authorities, who threw him into a dungeon with food that, in Porter's words, "Wasn't fit for dogs." He was now deep in enemy territory, where no one in the Church could come to his aid. Although he was formally charged with shooting Lilburn Boggs, the real reason for his imprisonment was to snare Joseph Smith. It was the beginning of a long ordeal that would challenge the resolve of even Porter Rockwell.[26]

26 Rockwell gave details of his arrest, imprisonment, and eventual release and return to Nauvoo. Those details are summarized in this and the next five chapters. (See *History of the Church* 6:135–42.)

PORTER AND THE JAILBREAK

IT DIDN'T TAKE LONG FOR Porter to come to despise the jail in Independence. Unfortunately, it became his home for the next nine months. The place was deplorable, with vermin to torment and irritate his skin, food that was practically inedible, and no fires allowed, even in the damp and cold weather. He also said that his only bed was a pile of filthy straw. Speaking of the food, Porter told a friend, "What I wouldn't eat one day was given to me the next until it was gone." In these conditions Porter began to lose weight, even though he was fairly trim to begin with.

At night he was handcuffed in the dungeon, but during the morning he was allowed into an upper cell until he received his one meal a day, at noon. As soon as his meager meal was finished, it was back to the dungeon.

After a number of months in these conditions, he was getting quite skinny and decided that he had to make an escape to save his life. After studying the situation carefully in his mind, he struck upon a plan. He got the idea that when he was locked in the dungeon, the door to the upper cell was left unlocked. If this was true, then the key to escape was to get out of the dungeon and into the upper room. To do this he decided to carefully remove the stovepipe to the unused potbellied stove in his dungeon cell. Once the stovepipe was out of the way, he was skinny enough that he could fit through the opening that the pipe extended through, getting into the upper cell when it was abandoned.

When the time was right, in the middle of the night, he assumed the jailer was dozing off because he knew Porter was locked securely in the dungeon. Porter made his first attempt as carefully and quietly as he could, working away on the stovepipe until he was able to detach it from the stove and pull it down from the ceiling of the dungeon. Sure enough, there was moonlight coming in through the open window in the upper cell. Next, he took off his shirt and wedged himself through the small hole into the upper cell room. Freedom was just one door away. But as he made his way in the darkness to the door, he found to his chagrin that the door was locked. If he was caught in the upper cell, they would know that he was attempting an escape, and he feared they would never allow him into that cell again—consigning him to the dungeon for as long as they cared to keep him. Desperate not to let that happen, he threw his clothes back down through the hole into the dungeon and shimmied his way down through the hole and back into the dreaded dungeon. He carefully replaced the stovepipe and did everything possible to conceal his activities. Of course that wasn't such a problem since no one, including the jailer, wanted to come into the dungeon to inspect him.

The next night he made a second attempt. He again made it into the upper cell only to find the door was again locked. Desperate to get out, he took the handle off a pail that was stored in a corner of the upper cell and tried to jimmy the lock, but he was unsuccessful in the attempt. But undaunted, he kept working at it so long that he got quite sleepy and then decided to close his eyes for a few minutes before trying again. Sure enough, he fell sound asleep in the upper cell, where he was discovered by the jailer the next morning.

His captors decided to handcuff his right hand to his left foot and his left hand to his right foot in such a position that he could not sit up straight. It must have been excruciating to pass the days and nights in this uncomfortable and unhealthy position.

As the days, weeks, and months passed away, Porter was growing more frail, the chance increasing that he would simply die in jail from malnutrition and lack of physical activity. One day, a new prisoner was introduced into the jail—a counterfeiter who became Porter's new jail mate. The jailer didn't search this man very well, but Porter did. In doing so, he discovered a file tucked away in the man's boot, which Porter quickly confiscated. Porter immediately went to work filing through the metal in his shackles and handcuffs. It was slow, tedious work, but Porter was nothing if not determined, and after a couple of days of concealing this activity from the jailer, he was ready. When the jailer opened the door to the cell to bring in their noonday meal, Porter lunged at the jailer and shoved him to a corner while the counterfeiter rushed past both of them and through the open door, down the stairs, and out into the yard. Keeping his wits about him, even while escaping, Porter grabbed the keys from the door and locked it with the jailer inside and then threw the keys out an open window. Then he too bounded down the stairs.

His timing was off, though, because the jailer's wife had heard the ruckus and emerged from their apartment in the lower floor of the jail just in time for Porter to collide with her. Rather than keep going, he bent down and helped her up, apologizing as he did so. "I haven't hurt your husband—he's locked in the cell. The keys are in the garden—I threw them out the window. But I am breaking jail, so I have to be going." With that, Porter bolted through the front door of the jail and made a run for freedom. Even though he was delayed by all the activity in the jail, he managed to overtake the counterfeiter as he sprinted up to the last remaining obstacle between him and freedom, a very tall fence. One biographer has written that it was twelve feet high, but whatever the height, Porter was able to scale it, even in his emaciated condition. He jumped down to the other side where he had a clear shot for a heavily wooded area where he could disappear into the trees.

Then he heard the cry, "Help! Help!" Turning back, he heard the counterfeiter struggling on the front side of the fence. Of course he could have left him, but it was the counterfeiter's file that had helped them gain their freedom, so Porter decided to help him. Climbing back up and over the fence, he jumped down, got beneath the counterfeiter, and started to boost him over the fence. Then, to his dread, he felt the cold metal barrel of a pistol jabbed into his neck. Sheriff Reynolds, having been alerted by the noise of the escape, had managed to intercept them. Porter let the counterfeiter down and turned to face the sheriff, who promptly handcuffed the two prisoners with their hands in front of them and ordered them back to jail.

By this point the townspeople were up in arms about the jailbreak, and a group of local barflies quickly formed a mob to lynch Porter. As the sheriff and his two prisoners arrived at the jail, they were met by this group of ruffians who were jeering and demanding justice. The sheriff took one look at this group, hesitated for a moment, and then shoved Porter into the midst of them, shouting, "Do with him as you . . . please!"

Unfortunately for the man with the noose, he tried to put it around Porter's neck. In spite of his handcuffs, Porter managed to wrestle the noose away from the man and beat him senseless with it. He shook the noose at the other men and said in very explicit words exactly what he would do to any man who dared to lay a hand on him. Just as Moses parted the Red Sea, Porter had so successfully intimidated the men in the mob that they fell back, creating a corridor for Porter and the counterfeiter to make their way to the jail cell, where Porter locked himself in for safety.

The jailbreak was a failure, but at least he lived to see another day—one in which he could insult and taunt his Missouri neighbors.[27]

---

27 While Porter was imprisoned in Independence, the Prophet Joseph prophesied that his friend would get away honorably from his captors. (See *History of the Church* 5:305.)

Porter Goes Fishing While in Jail

A PROTESTANT MINISTER AND HIS family lived across the street from the jail, and the minister's daughter befriended Porter, perhaps in the name of Christian charity. It turned out to be a godsend for the beleaguered Porter, since she periodically brought him hot coals to warm him up a bit and even food on occasion, including corn dodgers. A corn dodger is a hard corn biscuit that was an excellent source of nutrition on the frontier.

One day, as Porter studied a corn dodger, he asked his young friend to bring him a fishing pole, some line, and a hook. He told her that his intent was to fish for pike in the small stream running below the window of the upper cell.

Well, it really wasn't all that practical of an idea, particularly since Porter would sometimes dangle the line with a dodger on it at eye level. He was pleased that it amused the local minister and his family, as well as the neighborhood children, to see a fishing line hanging out the second-story window of a jail cell. At the very least it made him feel a little less isolated.

On one particular day Porter saw a group of men coming, so he stuck his fishing pole out the window with the dodger at eye level just as they happened by.

"Rockwell, what are you doing up there?" one fellow finally called out.

"Fishing for PUKES!" Porter shouted back cheerfully.

Well, this had the desired effect, for the term *puke* was a derisive term used by Illinois citizens when speaking of Missourians. Even though he was a former resident of Missouri, Porter was now a resident of the Illinois side of the river and so he chose this phrase—a clever play on the word *pike*—to insult the men below.

The fellow at the base stuttered for a moment and then called back, "Have you caught any lately?"

"No, but I've some glorious nibbles!"

JOSEPH PROPHESIES FOR PORTER

WHILE PORTER LANGUISHED IN A Missouri jail, worried for his friend Joseph Smith, his mother was back in Nauvoo trying to figure out ways to help her son get the defense he needed to stand trial. She went to the Prophet Joseph and asked him for money to pay for Porter's defense, but he had to confess that he didn't have any money.

By a strange coincidence at exactly this same time a grand jury was finally convened in Independence, Missouri, to hear the facts relative to Porter's charges. When the case was laid out before the jury, including the lack of eyewitnesses and Porter's sworn affidavits that he was hundreds of miles away at the time—with nothing to contradict his statements—the grand jury refused to bring charges, essentially telling the prosecution that they couldn't bring charges against him for attempting to kill Boggs because there was no credible evidence to say that he did. But the authorities kept Porter in jail anyway, because he remained their primary lure to get their hands on Joseph Smith.

Back in Nauvoo, Joseph felt bad that he couldn't personally help Porter and expressed that to Porter's mother. Then he brightened and said, "Come with me." Taking her by the arm, he and she walked together up the hill to the site where the magnificent new temple was under construction. Climbing on one of the giant granite stones, he started waving his hat while yelling for the workers to gather around. As the work on the temple ground to a halt, the men finally gathered together, and Joseph Smith called out, "Does Napoleon have a friend in the

French army?"[30] That got their attention. Then he proceeded to tell them of Porter's plight and passed his hat around for donations. The hat came back full. Joseph Smith and Sarah Rockwell thanked the men and then made their way down to the center of Nauvoo.

Apparently there was some kind of a carnival going on at the time, and Joseph got there as the wrestling event was being held. Seizing the opportunity, Joseph challenged the biggest, strongest man in the crowd. That brought out the bets, with the odds resting on the big fellow. Once again a hat was passed and quickly filled as people gathered eagerly to see this momentous contest between their moderately sized spiritual leader and his Goliath-sized opponent. When the referee's arm dropped, Joseph Smith proceeded to soundly beat the fellow, finishing the match with a flourish by picking the man up by his collar and the seat of the pants and throwing him head over heels into a ditch. As the man spluttered in the water, Joseph extended his hand and pulled him out, apologizing for being so rough with him. But Joseph had won the prize money fair and square.[31]

Between the money donated by the workers at the temple site and the prize money earned in the wrestling match, Joseph now had $200 to give to Porter's mother. Before she left for Independence, the Prophet made a prophecy, which was recorded at the time, that Porter would be honorably released from his persecutors in Missouri. With both money for his defense and a prophecy to sustain her, Sarah Rockwell set out once again for Missouri.

---

30 *Wandle Mace, Journal.* "Mace Recounted the Scene at the Temple," 92.
31 The story of the wrestling match was printed in *Juvenile Instructor,* vol. 27, 892.

ALEXANDER DONOVAN
DEFENDS PORTER

Without the grand jury's indictment, the Missourians were frustrated in their attempt to hold Porter any longer until an enterprising fellow came up with the idea to try him for his attempted jailbreak. Fortunately, Porter's mother arrived back in Independence just in time to use the $200 raised by Joseph Smith to hire him a lawyer. With that much money, he had his pick of anyone he wanted. Wisely, he chose an old friend of the Mormons, Alexander Donovan. Donovan was the member of the state legislature who had earlier worked to find a county that could be settled exclusively by the Mormons and who had refused to summarily execute Joseph Smith when he was arrested on charges of sedition.

On the charge of breaking out of jail there really was no defense—Porter was clearly guilty. But Donovan convinced the jury that it was a justified attempt, given his unjust imprisonment and unconstitutional delay in his right to a fair and expedient trial, so they convicted Porter and sentenced him to five minutes. Even in those dark days, there were fair-minded people, even in Missouri.

The prosecution team was furious and delayed for another five hours while they tried to think up new charges against Porter—that's how desperate they were to keep him as their pawn in getting to Joseph Smith. Finally Donovan convinced the court that they had to release Porter Rockwell.

Porter and his mother were left to make their way back to Nauvoo in the middle of December without any assistance. Donovan warned Porter that there was "a plot out to kill you, so don't take the traveled roads." Frustrated by all that had happened, Porter ignored Donovan's well-intentioned warning, and he and his mother started walking down the main route out of town. Once out in the country, they heard men approaching on horses. Porter quickly diverted off the path and helped his mother hide in snow-covered bushes. As the men came to the spot, they paused, and Porter and Sarah held their breath as they heard one of the men say, "He hasn't been gone too long. He should be here somewhere." Fortunately, Porter was skilled enough in backcountry stalking that he had left no trail to alert the marauders, and the men continued down the main road.

So now Porter and Sarah had to make their way through the thick underbrush in the dead of winter. Anyone who has been to Missouri can attest to how thick the trees and scrub brush are and how difficult it would be to trailblaze through such a hostile environment. But Porter's instincts were true, and eventually they made their way through the forest to a friendly farmhouse, where they were allowed to spend the evening. The next day, Porter gave most of what money he had left to his mother to take a coach back to Nauvoo. When she protested that she didn't want to leave him, he insisted that it was too dangerous for her to travel with him. So reluctantly she went into town and paid the fare to take a stagecoach back to Nauvoo.

Porter was left to find his own way out of Missouri. When he later related his story to friends, he said that he made his way by walking for great periods, sometimes as much as twenty-five miles per day. Occasionally he was lucky enough to find a friendly farmer who would allow him to borrow or rent a horse to carry him for an agreed-upon distance. With the farmer's son on the back of the horse, so he could return it after the allotted period, Porter would cover a far greater distance with much less difficulty. But it wasn't always possible to find a friendly face in the wilds, and so Porter was left to walk much of the distance on his own. On one occasion he became so overwhelming fatigued that he asked a fellow traveler going the same direction if he would take fifty cents to carry him piggyback as far as the fellow could go. The man accepted this unusual offer and carried Porter on his back. By this time Porter's feet were worn thin and bleeding.

After more than 275 miles, covered in eleven tortuous days, Porter Rockwell finally arrived in Nauvoo on Christmas Day. What a sight he must have made. He hadn't had a change of clothing in the nine months since he had been arrested, his long black hair and beard untrimmed.

PORTER'S DRAMATIC ENTRANCE
AND BLESSING

AFTER SPENDING ELEVEN DAYS IN the wild traveling under tremendous adversity, it seemed the perfect time to call on Joseph Smith, who was hosting a party at the Mansion House. Finding his way to the Mansion House, and observing the goings-on through the windows, Porter made his way to the door, where he loudly interrupted the guests at that end of the house. Alarmed, someone called out that a drunk was trying to break into the party. Joseph yelled out to the guards, "Throw that drunken Missourian out." That phrase gives a little insight into how the Mormons felt about the Missourians, doesn't it?

Unfortunately, the guards couldn't throw this particular Missourian out because he was stronger than all of them. That aggravated Joseph to where he took off his coat to do the job himself. Making his way to that end of the hall, Joseph grabbed the stranger by his shoulder and, just before going after him, happened to peer into those utterly distinctive, steel-gray eyes. He saw a big smile under the thick mustache and realized with a great roar of laughter that it was Porter, playing one of his old tricks. Delighted, the Prophet brought him into the room and sat him on a chair and then asked everyone to gather around to listen to Porter tell the story of his being captured, imprisoned, and finally acquitted and allowed to return to Nauvoo in such an awful condition. In his usual straightforward way, Porter described all the events that had kept him separated from the Saints for all the time he'd been on the lam, and then captured in St. Louis, and the travails he'd suffered in Independence.

As the story drew to its conclusion, there was no laughter in the room. The Prophet was so moved by Porter's story that he gave him a blessing right on the spot, with a house full of witnesses. He placed his hands on Porter's shoulders and promised him in absolute and unmistakable language that as "long as he was true and faithful to his covenants, to the Church, and to his God, that no bullet or blade would ever harm him." Everyone who heard this interpreted it the same way—that no man could kill him. As a token of his acceptance of this promise, he was never to cut his hair again. This was a sacred and solemn pledge and one that would change Porter's life forever. It would give him the confidence to face the many life-threatening situations that would present themselves to Porter individually and the Saints as a whole. It is unique in modern history and a defining aspect of the life and legend of Porter Rockwell.

Although it wasn't recorded, the Prophet also was said to have counseled Porter never to cut his beard. Associated with that token was a promise that Porter would have the gift of healing. Many lives would be blessed because the Prophet Joseph Smith bestowed this unique spiritual gift of healing to Porter Rockwell.

Porter was home. The Prophet was overjoyed, and Sarah Rockwell was at peace for the first time in nine months. Joseph's earlier prophecy that Porter would be honorably released from jail had been fulfilled.[32]

---

32 The Prophet Joseph comments on Porter's return to Nauvoo (see *History of the Church* 6:134–35). He did not, however, record the blessing given to Rockwell, even though Porter often told his children of the blessing.

PORTER'S FIRST SALOON— THE MANSION HOUSE

PORTER WAS HOME AND FREE of the Missourians, with no outstanding warrants or judgments against him. His mother was caring for his children, who were thrilled to have their father back. That was the good news. The bad news was that his wife had divorced him and he was absolutely penniless. Joseph took pity on him and devised a plan to give Porter employment.

While Emma was off to St. Louis to buy furniture for the Mansion House, Joseph decided to install a fully stocked bar in the Mansion House. That would make it far easier to entertain guests and make them comfortable. So while Emma was away he had carpenters build the bar and then proudly announced that Porter was to be the bartender.

When Emma returned from her shopping expedition, she entered her home through the front door, and the first thing she saw was Porter Rockwell standing there with a nice new black coat on, a stylish black hat, white shirt, and a black string tie, busily polishing a whiskey glass or two. Emma was not amused and made it clear to Joseph with words to this effect: "Either that goes," referring to the bar, "or the children and I will never set foot in this house again."

Joseph made his decision quickly. "Yes, dear, I'll have it removed immediately."

Witnessing this exchange, Porter knew he was unemployed again. He also witnessed yet again the strength of Emma's personality.[33]

---

33 Note from John Rockwell: A number of years ago, I took my family to Nauvoo, Illinois, to visit the sites where my great-great-grandfather lived. Knowing of this story, I was brazen enough to ask the young lady who was serving as our guide in the Mansion House, "Where was the bar?" I wasn't sure she would know the story, but she did. "It was right over there." I was very pleased to verify the truth of

Joseph didn't abandon Porter in his search for employment. Instead he helped set him up in two new businesses. The first thing he did was buy Porter a carriage and two matching black horses so he could run a livery service in Nauvoo. The second was to deed to him the property just to the side of the Mansion House on the side closest to the Mississippi River so that Porter could build an inn and a barber shop. Having been commanded by the Prophet to never cut his hair, Porter Rockwell owning a barber shop was a notable irony. As for the saloon, it ended up being exiled from the Mansion House, even though it was still built next door.

---

this story and made my way to the spot. I hoped to have my picture taken there, but that was not allowed. Still, as I stood where the bar was, I had a peculiar and moving reaction, realizing that I was standing where my great-great-grandfather had stood at a very difficult time in his life. It was an experience I enjoyed very much.

THE *NAUVOO EXPOSITOR*

Porter's happiness at his return to the fellowship of the Saints was all too short-lived. By selecting the site for Nauvoo in a worthless swamp on the Illinois side of the Mississippi River, Church leaders had hoped that they would not arouse the ire or envy of their neighbors. They were tired of persecution and longed for the chance to establish Zion without interference or harassment. But it wasn't to be. Perhaps the greatest disappointment to Joseph Smith was that much of the persecution in Nauvoo arose from within the Church itself, with the most adamant critics finding their voice after being expelled from the Church.

The beginning of the end for Joseph Smith came when the Law brothers and the Higby brothers, once holding high positions of leadership within the Church but now excommunicated, began a newspaper to expose Joseph as a fallen prophet. They named their newspaper the *Nauvoo Expositor,* and it was incendiary in its accusations against Joseph Smith and the Church. Once the outrageous claims and charges published in the paper became intolerable to Joseph Smith, he took action in his role as mayor of the city to have the paper destroyed. While he may have been justified in doing so, the consequences were tragic.

While it seems incredible that American citizens would set out to destroy a newspaper, given our high regard for freedom of the press, it was hardly without precedence in frontier America. The Missourians had destroyed more than one Mormon press while the Saints lived in that state. But the reason that the destruction of the *Nauvoo Expositor* caused such a ruckus had to do with an abolitionist preacher named Elijah P. Lovejoy, who had come to Illinois some years earlier to start an antislavery newspaper. Those in favor of slavery took exception to his newspaper and decided to destroy the press. In doing so, they accidentally killed the minister and the editor. This action caused a firestorm of criticism, both in Illinois and nationally, and so from that point forward the newspapers of Illinois had become sacred, with a universal hands-off policy. And now Joseph Smith, meeting with the Nauvoo City Council, decided to commit the very act that had aroused such ire and hostility in the earlier incident.

While the Prophet was directly responsible for ordering the destruction of the paper, Porter Rockwell kicked in the door and helped destroy the press. In doing so, he started the inevitable chain of events that would lead to the fulfillment of his worst and deepest fear, the martyrdom of the Prophet.

If My Life Has No Value
to My Friends

Perhaps the darkest night of Joseph Smith's life was when he and his brother Hyrum, along with Apostle Willard Richards, climbed into a leaky rowboat on the shores of the Mississippi River to cross from Nauvoo, Illinois, to the Iowa shore, where Joseph Smith hoped to make his way first to Washington DC to make another appeal to the federal government for protection and then to the valleys of the Rocky Mountains to once again establish the Church in lands so far removed from humankind that no one could "hurt or make afraid." At this point, Joseph still looked forward to his continued mortal life and to his role in the work of the Restoration. Later that evening he would understand that his time on earth was quickly drawing to an end.

Porter Rockwell was rowing the boat that night. The three passengers had spent the entire journey continuously bailing water to keep the boat from sinking while Porter rowed. Arriving on the western shore, Joseph was thoughtful for a time and then asked Porter to return to take a message to Emma Smith, as well as to go to work securing provisions and horses for the journey to Washington DC. Without questioning why Joseph hadn't asked this before their crossing, Porter immediately set out for Illinois.

He took Joseph's message to a very distressed Emma Smith. She did not like what she heard and told Porter that she wanted Joseph to return. She believed the governor would protect Joseph and Hyrum and felt that it was their place to be with the Saints. Reluctantly, Porter agreed to carry this message, perhaps knowing the emotional toll it would take on Joseph. Emma asked him to take Reynolds Cahoon, a local businessman and community leader, to help persuade Joseph to abandon his quest for the West. While some records suggest that Porter took Cahoon and two others with him, Cahoon is the only certainty. Accepting a personal letter from Emma, Porter led the party to the dock, where they once again boarded the boat for Iowa. Rowing across the river for the third time in one night is testament to Porter Rockwell's physical strength and endurance. But that was the least of his worries as they pulled up and signaled their arrival to Joseph, Hyrum, and Willard Richards.

Almost immediately Porter told Joseph of Emma's request, quickly followed by Reynolds Cahoon's heated allegation that to leave the Saints at this time would brand Joseph a coward who had abandoned his duty and his people. With his wife urging his return and Cahoon calling him a coward, Joseph uttered those hauntingly forlorn and poignant words, "If my life is of no value to my friends, it is of no value to me." These words, so reminiscent of, "Father, why hast Thou forsaken me," speak to the despair that Joseph must have felt.

Remembering the letter from Emma, Porter handed it to Joseph, who read it in silence. The contents of the letter are now lost to history, but Joseph looked up from it seeking advice. In the presence of two Apostles, one of whom was his brother, as well as Cahoon and perhaps others, Joseph first turned to Porter Rockwell. "What shall I do, Port?"

One can only imagine the anguish Porter Rockwell felt. "You are the oldest, Joseph, and you know what's best. You make your bed, and I will lie in it with you."

Joseph nodded and then turned to Hyrum. "What do you think?" Hyrum and Elder Richards said that they thought they should return, that the governor was honorable and would protect them. Joseph Smith accepted this judgment and motioned for the group to make its way to the river.

While the others hurried ahead, Joseph lingered to talk with Porter. No one knows what they said, but it took long enough that it apparently irritated Hyrum, for he turned and called to Joseph words to the effect of, "Come on, Joseph, hurry along!"

Joseph put his arm on Porter's shoulder and said quietly, "Why should I hurry? I am going to my death."

Porter was staggered by this. Struggling for words, he said, "If you want, Joseph, I'll gather the Saints one last time to hear you preach to them, by starlight if necessary." Joseph nodded, but it would not happen.

It was with heavy heart that Porter then rowed his way across the Mississippi River for the fourth time in a single evening. How many normal lifetimes had passed from those days in 1820 when a little boy of seven had pleaded for more time to listen to the words of the young man he idolized and loved—the man who he believed to be a prophet of God? There was no pine torch this benighted night—just the quiet lapping of the oars in the river as the condemned men bailed water on their way back to Carthage.

CARTHAGE

UPON RETURNING TO NAUVOO, JOSEPH indicated his willingness to submit to the charges leveled against him for his role in ordering the destruction of the newspaper. The authorities instructed that he be taken from Nauvoo to receive an impartial trial in the small town of Carthage, the county seat of Hancock County.

Joseph, Hyrum, and Willard Richards were given time to say good-bye to their families, and then they set off with their entourage. Joseph was not escorted by deputies or the militia but went on his own accord. Mounting their horses, the party started its way out of town. Before clearing the edge of the town, however, Joseph turned to Porter and said, "Porter, I want you to stay here in Nauvoo. I have some things I want you to do."

Porter protested, because he was Joseph's personal bodyguard, having said to Joseph when called to this position, "Joseph, your enemies are my enemies." He had always treated it that way. When Joseph repeated his order, Porter was perplexed. "Why would you want me to stay here in Nauvoo—I'm your bodyguard!"

"Well, I have things for you to do, so please stay behind." So Porter turned aside and watched with heavy heart as Joseph and the others plodded out of sight on their horses. He was one of the few who knew of Joseph's foreboding, having talked with him about it the previous night. Still, he must have had his doubts, because things had always worked out for Joseph before.

When the Prophet arrived in Carthage, he began a letter writing campaign trying to solicit any help he could possibly get.

Even in these desperate circumstances, he still took time to pen a letter to Porter, which a messenger took quickly back to Nauvoo. Porter had someone read the letter to him. It was ominous: "Under no circumstances are you to come to Carthage. If you do, you will be killed."[34] Once again the Prophet Joseph Smith took action to prevent his childhood friend from going to Carthage with him, because Joseph knew that Porter would die in the jail cell with him. Perhaps the Prophet knew there were other things Porter needed to accomplish to help the struggling Church in the years after Joseph's death.

We recall only briefly the events of Carthage Jail: the mournful singing of John Taylor as Joseph Smith struggled to find comfort and meaning in what was happening, the Carthage Grays who were charged with protecting the prisoners callously stepping aside as the mob stormed the building, the desperate struggle as the Prophet and Apostles fought desperately for their lives, and the heroic step into the window as Joseph Smith at last tried to save his friends by offering his own life.

Back in Nauvoo, Porter had been attending a meeting of the high council in which the various issues confronting the community, including Joseph's incarceration, were discussed. Porter left when the meeting was adjourned, determined that for the first time in his life he would defy Joseph and go to Carthage, regardless of the consequences. But as he got ready to leave, he discovered that he had left his hat behind in the room where the meeting had been held in the Mansion House. He decided that he couldn't go to Carthage without his hat, so he made his way back to the Mansion House to get it. He walked through the front door and made his way to the meeting room, quietly opening the door a crack to find that it was full of men, including Governor Ford. He clearly saw Ford sitting right in front of him, listening to a man who was talking. Rockwell heard this man say, "The deed is done before

---

34 *History of the Church* 6:565.

this time." Porter did not understand what these words meant, but they bothered him.[35] It can be assumed these men were discussing the completed murder of the Prophet Joseph Smith while sitting in his own home. Ford had promised to protect Joseph but instead had distanced himself from Carthage while knowing full well what result his complicity would yield.

While Porter didn't fully understand what had happened, he knew enough to be concerned for Joseph's life, and so he jumped on his horse and sped off for Carthage. As he galloped through the night, he was filled with dread. As he neared Carthage, he saw a man speeding toward him in a wagon on the road leading out of Carthage. He recognized the man, also a Mormon, and this man recognized Porter. But the frightened man was too frantic to stop and talk to Porter because he was being chased by a mob. As the man raced past Porter, he yelled out, "They've killed him. They've killed Joseph and Hyrum!"

By this point the mob was upon them, so Porter reined his horse to a stop, pulled out his rifle, and fired twice, killing two men in the mob, which caused the mob to wheel around and retreat. Porter, staggered by news of Joseph's death, spurred his horse around and raced back to Nauvoo.

Anson Call was the guard at the temple that night and would later recount the story of hearing a man racing up and down the streets of Nauvoo shouting. He didn't know who he was or what he was saying until he was a few blocks away. Then he recognized him. "It was Old Port, and he was shouting, 'They've killed him. They've killed Joseph. They've killed Hyrum! They've killed him!'"

---

35 *History of the Church* 6:588–89.

PORTER'S REVENGE

PORTER MADE A PROMISE THAT he would avenge the blood of Joseph Smith. But contrary to what many might expect of him, he didn't rush out and commit his own murders in a frenzy of revenge. A year after Joseph's assassination, Porter was caught up in an explosive situation that unexpectedly led to the fulfillment of his vow.

Brigham Young was leading the Church. The Saints were being threatened almost daily as the citizens of Illinois pushed to have them expelled from the state. In this hostile environment, Brigham called Porter in and asked him to pick a few other men to go out and help that night's victims of mob attacks—the ominously named "wolf hunts." So Porter picked a friend and off they went to bring aid to the victims. While they were resting their horses for a moment, a man came racing down the road on horseback going just as fast as his horse could go. When the man got close enough to recognize Porter, he reined his horse to a stop. It turns out that he was the local sheriff, Jacob Backenstos, and he deputized Porter on the spot. Once Porter was officially under his direction, Backenstos said to him, "You've got to protect my life. The Carthage Grays are out to kill me!"

Almost as if cued, the Carthage Grays emerged at the top of the hill, riding furiously after Backenstos. Porter said calmly, "Don't worry. I have my rifle, pistols, and seventy-two rounds of ammunition." Porter drew his rifle, aimed it carefully at the big silver belt buckle of the man who was leading the charge, and calmly pulled the trigger. The rider tumbled off the back of his horse, a dead man. The Carthage Grays pulled up to a stop and dismounted to collect their dead leader, and then they turned around and went the other way.

Porter was well aware of whom he had shot—it was Frank Worrell, leader of the Carthage Grays, the local militia assigned to protect Joseph Smith and the other prisoners while they were incarcerated in Carthage Jail. However, when the mob came to commit their murders, Worrell and his men had raised their weapons in the air, fired them harmlessly, and then coolly stepped out of the way so the mob could get to Joseph and Hyrum.

About this time, a local farmer came up to see what had happened, having heard the ruckus created by the mob attack and Porter's response to it, as well as the confusion which overtook the Grays as they withdrew down the road.

"What happened?" asked the farmer.

"I got him," replied Porter.

"Got who?"

"Frank Worrell. It was a far piece—didn't think I'd reach him."

With that Porter got on his horse and started back to Nauvoo. Along the way they encountered more mobs, and those in Porter's party shot and killed two more men in the mobs to protect the lives of the people who were being attacked. With Worrell's death Porter declared himself satisfied that he had avenged the blood of Joseph Smith by ending the life of the man who was supposed to protect the Prophet and the others but who allowed the murder to happen without resistance.[36]

---

36 George Washington Bean recounted Rockwell's shooting of Frank Worrell in his autobiography. See also *History of the Church* 7:446–47. It was stated that Rockwell had two "fifteen shooter rifles" in addition to pistols.

You Throw Rocks—
I'll Throw Lead

D URING THE YEAR FOLLOWING the Prophet's assassination there was a great deal of tension between the Mormons and non-Mormons in Illinois. Porter and a fellow member of the Church were out on the road delivering weapons to the Saints in the area when they stopped for dinner.

While they were eating, the townspeople realized that these two men were Mormons, and so they quickly devised a plan to stand by the side of the road and stone them when they left town.

When Porter and his friend finished their meal and stepped out to the wagon, it was obvious what the townspeople intended. Once in the wagon, Porter said to his friend, "You take the reins and are you ready?" The man said yes, and the wagon began to roll. Porter stood up in the wagon with rifle at his shoulder and shouted to the crowd, "The first one of you to throw a stone and I'll throw lead!"

The citizens stood dumbfounded at such audacity, and Porter and his friend rode safely out of town.

PORTER IS ENDOWED

IN TIME IT BECAME EVIDENT that the Saints would have to leave Nauvoo to protect their lives and livelihoods. To prepare them for the journey, Brigham Young urged all those who were able and available to continue working on the Nauvoo Temple so that he could officiate in the essential ordinances of the temple before the people were turned out of Nauvoo.

Porter had been called as a Seventy in the priesthood, and he was anxious to partake in the saving ordinances. So he went to the temple and received his own endowment. He then accepted an assignment to act as an officiator in the endowment ceremony. It will take some readers just a few seconds to figure out what role he played, but it's best to leave it at that. He was later to perform this same work in the Endowment House in Salt Lake City during the many years the Salt Lake Temple was under construction.

Porter was not able to participate in all the ordinances of the temple, since he was now divorced. His first wife's claim against Porter, when filing for divorce, was that he was more loyal to Joseph Smith than he was to her and that he was interested in polygamy. But Porter was never a polygamist. There are suggestions, by some critics, that at this point he took another man's wife to the temple to be sealed to him, even though she was legally married to her husband, Amos Davis. The sources for this claim are all anti-Mormon. One of the more notorious reports that supports this claim came from an anti-Mormon newspaper that claimed that Mrs. Davis was Porter's reward from Brigham Young for killing Frank Worrell. But after a thorough check of the temple records of the time and place where this was supposed to have taken place, there are absolutely no records of Porter Rockwell being sealed to a Mrs. Davis—nor to any other women. He was a divorced single parent.

PORTER'S NEW CALLING

EVEN THOUGH THE MISSISSIPPI RIVER filled with Mormons leaving Illinois in the most desperate of circumstances, the anti-Mormons were not satisfied. Mobs continued to harass those who were left behind while the initial refugees made their way to Winter Quarters, Nebraska.

During these early days of the exodus, Porter was enlisted as a messenger for Brigham Young. Records indicate that he made his way back and forth across Iowa at least five times in this service.

Try to put yourself in Porter's shoes. You've just made it into Winter Quarters, having crossed the Iowa yet again, when you're called into Brigham Young's log cabin. Then you hear these words: "Brother Rockwell, I have an assignment for you. Brother Rockwell, we've left some good Saints behind. They're poor. They weren't ready and now they're being harassed mercilessly by the mobs. Now would you mind going back and getting yourself arrested for killing Frank Worrell so that it will take the attention of the mobs off those good Saints and put it on you?" Porter had been in prison before, in Independence, Missouri, and it had nearly killed him. But Brigham Young continued: "Now I promise to get you a good lawyer." That was the extent of his assurance. Many would hesitate, but not Porter. He had accepted Brigham's role as leader of the Church, and he now consented to carry out this remarkable assignment.

First, word was sent ahead of his impending arrival back in Nauvoo. When Porter showed up in town, he checked into a boarding house and then went outside looking for an opportunity to cause some trouble that would draw attention. He soon found an old enemy of his whom he started chasing around the streets of Nauvoo while firing his pistols over the poor man's head. It didn't take very long for this to attract the attention of the local law officers, who started chasing him. Porter retreated to his boarding house, where he boarded himself up. The local Saints, who were aware of the plan, played this up to the sheriff. "Rockwell's in town, and he's going to cause us problems." In their public meetings they even condemned Porter as a loose cannon.

With even the Mormons apparently against Porter, the sheriff felt emboldened to take action. Porter's reputation had preceded him, so the sheriff rather prudently waited until he could assemble a posse to storm the boarding house. After three hours of negotiations, Porter finally surrendered and came out the front door. With his arms raised above his head, the sheriff moved to disarm him, in the process retrieving from Porter a double-barrel sawed-off shotgun tied under his coat on one side of his body, a second shotgun on the other side, two Bowie knives, a pair of Colt revolvers, and enough spare cylinders preloaded in his coat pockets that he could have easily shot over seventy times without having had to pause to reload.

Porter was taken off to prison and assigned a lawyer: Almon Babbitt, the same man who happened to be his first wife's divorce lawyer. Talk about irony. Porter Rockwell was rather serene about the whole situation because he felt he was called to this situation by Brigham Young, the prophet of God.

In his earlier imprisonment in Independence, Porter was anxious to get the trial started and ended. In this case he intended to drag it out, since every day spent in jail with his name in the newspapers and the non-Mormons stirred up against him was one day less persecution for the poor Saints preparing for the journey West. As it turned out, he spent four months in jail awaiting trial.

When the trial finally began, his lawyer turned out to be a very good defender. His primary strategy for Porter's defense was to summon Sheriff Jacob Backenstos to testify on Porter's behalf. Backenstos explained that he had deputized Porter and then testified under oath that, "I ordered Porter to shoot to defend my life."

When both the prosecution and defense rested their case, the jury was excused to deliberate Porter's fate. He was accused of a capital crime, which would carry with it the death sentence. But when the jurors reassembled in the courtroom, they rendered their verdict: "innocent by virtue of self-defense." Porter was a free man, completely exonerated of his actions in defending the Saints in those earlier days.

When Porter left the courtroom, he made his way to the Mansion House. Standing on the street across from Joseph Smith's last home, he pondered the events of the life he had spent with this remarkable man.

While standing here, Porter failed, at first, to see a figure approaching him. It was Joseph Smith III, the son of the Prophet Joseph Smith. When the young man recognized Porter, he ran up to him and leaped into his arms. Porter was overcome with emotion, and with tears streaming down his eyes and onto his face and beard, he said to the young thirteen-year-old boy, "Oh, Joseph, Joseph, they killed the only friend I ever had!"

The young man tried to comfort him, but Porter eventually had to say, "Now it's not safe to be seen with me—you better go in the house with your mother." With that they said good-bye, never to meet again.

Years later, when Joseph Smith III was the president of the Reorganized Church of Jesus Christ of Latter Day Saints, he was interviewed by a newspaper reporter who asked what he knew about his father's old friend, Porter Rockwell. Joseph Smith's son had only good things to say about Porter Rockwell, attesting to what a great friend he had been to their family.[37]

---

37 At the time of Rockwell's arrest for shooting Frank Worrell, Hosea Stout believed some treachery had taken place or Rockwell wouldn't have been captured. One newspaper at the time, the *Quincy Whig,* May 13, 1846, even expressed some sympathy for Rockwell. While Rockwell was in jail for four months awaiting trial in the Worrell shooting, the Mormon Battalion was called to serve in the Mexican-American War. If he had been back in Illinois in jail, he most likely would have been called to serve in the army.

PORTER IN THE WEST

PORTER ON HIS OWN

IN THE NEXT THIRTY-ONE YEARS, Porter would stand on his own, no longer a protégé of Joseph Smith, but a force to be reckoned with in his own right. He chose to stay with the main branch of the Church, becoming a loyal advisor to Brigham Young. Brigham Young sought his advice on a number of key issues, at one point stating that Porter was the only man whose judgment regarding the Indians he fully trusted.

In the vastness of the West, his reputation would take on bigger-than-life proportions, with myths abounding about his exploits that either demonized him or lionized him, depending on who was telling the story.

In the post-Nauvoo period, Porter crisscrossed the Great Plains on numerous occasions while in service to the Church. He also opened the road from Utah to Southern California while checking up on the Mormon Battalion for Brigham Young. He traveled the road to Sacramento in northern California on a similar assignment to help collect the tithing of the Mormons who had traveled on the sailing ship *Brooklyn,* lingering for a while to serve the needs of the forty-niners who worked the California gold fields. Back in Utah he was appointed a deputy marshal and ended up serving for the rest of his life. He also married two more times, consecutively, not in plural marriage, and raised more children. For a time he made his home in Lehi, where he operated inns, stables, and livery service. He also worked for Wells Fargo and the U.S. Army.

PORTER IN THE VANGUARD

AFTER BEING ACQUITTED FOR THE death of Frank Worrell, Porter made his way to Winter Quarters, Nebraska, where he was introduced to Brigham Young's newest plan. Brigham planned to take about one hundred men and a limited number of women to form a vanguard group to scout out a new home for the Saints in the West. They intended to leave the boundaries of the United States for what was then Mexican and unclaimed land west of the Louisiana Purchase. Before proceeding, Brigham asked Porter to be his lead scout and hunter for the party. Porter accepted and became the individual who scouted the famous Mormon Trail.

Out on the plains there were far too many stories to recount. A number stand out, though, both for what they say about Porter and what they reveal about the trials of the trail.

Brigham Young had a favorite spyglass that he used to survey the land. He lost it one day and became upset at its loss, so much so that the men in the party couldn't stand his constant complaining about it. When Porter had finally had enough of Brigham's ill temper, he decided to do something about it. Porter turned his horse around and retraced the trail they had been following. A few days later Porter rode into camp and ceremoniously presented the spyglass to Brigham Young, who sputtered his appreciation, and everything was calm after that.

For his part, Porter didn't need a spyglass, since he was known for his keen eyesight. In some instances he could spot a distant landmark as much as a day or two before other people in the party could see it with their unaided eye.

On another occasion a group of Indians had stolen some horses. So Brigham said to Porter, "Get some men and go get the horses back."

After some skillful tracking, they found the guilty Indians, but they were on foot with no horses. The Indians begged them for tobacco. But Porter did not use tobacco—their chances might have been a lot better if they'd asked him for whiskey, but they were out of luck with tobacco. As they were talking with the Indians, another group of Indians appeared on the brow of a gully, galloping directly toward them, firing their guns and shooting a cascade of arrows at Porter and his men. There had to be at least a dozen in this new group, and the Indians who were walking immediately hit the ground. It appeared that the Indians on the horses had stolen the horses from the Indians on foot, who had originally stolen them from the Mormons.

Porter had three of his own men to protect, so he dropped the reins over his saddle horn, took out two pistols, spurred his horse, and charged the Indians head-on. The Indians had a healthy respect for bravery, and as soon as they saw this wild-looking white man with unshaven beard and uncut hair charging at them, guns blazing, they heeled around and took off. Charging with guns ablaze became Porter Rockwell's trademark.

Another day found Porter hunting for buffalo with a man named Henson Walker Jr. He was a prominent farmer in Nauvoo, and he and Porter were friends.[38] As they were talking, Porter recounted a legend he'd heard from an old mountain man that claimed you can't kill a buffalo by shooting it between the eyes because the hide and skull are just too thick for a bullet to

---

38 John Rockwell Note: Seemingly insignificant events have lasting consequences. Years after this, Henson Walker's great-great-great-granddaughter would become my wife, thus joining the two families together. When our oldest son, named Orrin Porter Rockwell, got engaged, his fiancée, Julie Marie Gunther called the temple to reserve a date. When asked who she was marrying she replied, "Orrin Porter Rockwell." Silence. Then, "Is this a joke?" It was not, but we've enjoyed talking about it ever since.

penetrate. Porter wanted to either prove or disprove this theory, so when they came upon a large herd of buffalo, Porter fired a pistol to stampede the herd. Then, to the astonishment of Henson Walker, Porter dropped his reins over the saddle horn and, using his feet to guide his horse, charged out to the side of the stampeding buffalo to get ahead of the lead bull. His horse was quick and surefooted, and in time Porter was able to overtake the animal. Working his way ahead of it, he pulled out his rifle, threw it over his shoulder, and pulled the trigger. The ball hit the buffalo right between the eyes. The stunned animal locked his legs as he screeched to a halt, paused to look up at the man who had just taken a shot at him, and then proceeded to chase Porter all the way back to the wagon train, where someone shot the bull. The legend was proved true.

Under the leadership of Brigham Young and the skillful scouting of Porter Rockwell, the vanguard company survived this initial trek across the wilderness, where they ultimately arrived at the summit of East Canyon above the Great Salt Lake valley. Porter had guided the camp to the very spot Brigham Young was anxious to explore.[39]

---

39 The stories of the Indians, the spyglass, and the buffalo hunt are found in William Clayton's journal.

EARLY DAYS IN UTAH

UTAH IN 1847 WAS CALLED a godforsaken place by non-Mormons. Brigham Young and his followers saw it differently, viewing it as a God-preserved haven from their enemies, although God left much of the work of turning it into a habitable place up to the hard work of the Saints.

When Brigham Young's wagon train pulled up to the mouth of Emigration Canyon, Wilford Woodruff later reported that he turned the carriage so that President Young could see the whole valley. While looking out across the valley, Brigham Young was given a vision that lasted for several minutes, and on this occasion he reported that he saw the future glory of Zion as they would grow in strength and success in this valley. He prophesied that the Saints would fill the entire valley from north to south and east to west with a great city that would be the envy of the world. When the vision passed, he declared, "It is enough. This is the right place. Drive on."[40]

While no one can say for certain, Porter Rockwell was the lead scout, so it's quite possible that Porter Rockwell was the first Mormon to enter the Salt Lake valley, since Brigham Young was sick on that day.

In the course of the next few years, Brigham Young sent Porter off on a variety of assignments that included exploring the valleys in northern Utah, going back on the Mormon Trail to help bring a wagon train in, and even joining Brigham Young in traveling back to Winter Quarters.

One of the best stories about Porter occurred on his trip back to Nebraska with Brigham Young. Porter was awakened

---

one night at the sound of a group of Sioux Indians stealing most of their horses while they were asleep. Not bothering to wake the rest of the men, Porter sneaked off in the dead of night and made his way on foot to the Indians' camp, where he was able to quietly retrieve some of their horses without the Sioux being aware of it. The horses were vital to the safety of the Mormon party since it was winter, and without these horses they would have had to walk. Had the Indians succeeded, Brigham's party may have frozen to death without their horses.

On another occasion, back in the Salt Lake valley and in better weather, Brigham Young asked Porter to take a pack train full of trade goods and to visit all the Indians around the valley to offer them gifts to keep the peace. That particular calling took up a full spring, summer, and autumn, but it gave Porter a chance to become friends with many of the area's Indians and to gain their trust. It was an effort that would benefit the Saints and Porter for years to come.

Life on the trail and in the desert was lonely, and upon returning to Salt Lake City at the end of his assignment, Porter happened to meet up with the Neff family that he had met in one of the wagon trains coming across the plains. John Neff had a lovely young daughter named Mary Ann who caught Porter's eye. He started to court her and was pleased that she returned his affection. Porter and Mary Ann were sealed together in the parlor of Brigham Young's home, since there was no temple or even an endowment house yet. Hosting the wedding was a very generous act on Brigham Young's part, although he probably owed it to Porter since he sent him out on a new Church assignment the very next day that separated him from his new bride.

Because of Porter's unique ability with the Indians in Utah, Brigham Young sent Porter to visit the chief of one of the Ute Indian tribes. He was accompanied by George Washington Bean, a young man who was quick to pick up Indian languages.

Their goal was to conclude a peace treaty with the Utes in the Nephi area, some seventy-five miles south of Salt Lake City.

During this busy time, Porter was not too busy to accept public office. In the first open election held in the Salt Lake valley, Sheriff Hayward was elected and immediately deputized Porter as his deputy marshal for the Territory of Deseret. As noted earlier, it must have been an appointment for life since he held that post until his death.

Porter's life in Utah was varied and interesting. He became a rancher and a businessman. He secured mail contracts which paid him to see the U.S. Mail carried safely through the territory, among other jobs. He also played a role in California, where immigration was gaining momentum and where Porter took a leading role in entering into contracts for the Church.

PORTER IN CALIFORNIA

A S BRIGHAM YOUNG ATTEMPTED TO consolidate the main body of the Church into Salt Lake City, it was important for him to stay in touch with the groups scattered about the country. There were groups of members still making their way from Illinois and crossing Iowa. There were boatloads of immigrants arriving from England—generally traveling to New Orleans and then up the Mississippi and Missouri Rivers to Winter Quarters before embarking on the 1,300-mile trek to Utah. Still other groups went round South America by ship and up to San Francisco and then across the Nevada and Utah desert. It was a vast undertaking no matter what the route.

But one of the most important groups for Brigham Young to track was the Mormon Battalion. Their wages had been paid directly to Brigham Young by the Army, which is the main way the prophet financed the great migration to the West. The Church was always in desperate need of money because they essentially had to start from scratch in building up a new community once again, having lost their property in Missouri and Illinois. Even though the services of the battalion helped finance Church expenses, the battalion also sapped the Saints of many able-bodied men. Brigham Young was anxious to have the battalion's soldiers returned to them as soon as possible.

One day Brigham summoned Porter to act as guide for a party under the leadership of Jefferson Hunt that was headed for San Diego to check up on the members of the Mormon Battalion and to make some contracts on behalf of the Church. Porter agreed and essentially blazed a new trail from Salt Lake

City through what is now Utah, Nevada, and California. Once in San Diego, Porter made quite a name for himself and successfully negotiated the contracts Brigham Young desired, including the purchase of a large order of beef cattle. On the return trip, Porter and Jefferson Hunt parted ways, and Porter was able to keep all of the animals under his control alive and healthy, even in the harsh and arid environment they passed through. Jefferson Hunt, on the other hand, lost almost half the cattle under his control. Porter was the first person to successfully bring wagons into Utah along the southern route on the Old Spanish Trail.

After mustering out of the army in San Diego, many members of the Mormon Battalion[41] went by ship to San Francisco, where they worked as laborers to earn money. When James Marshall discovered gold at Sutter's Mill near Sacramento, starting the famous 1849 gold rush, these Church members moved into the gold fields. Brigham Young wanted to stay in touch, so he sent Porter and Apostle Amasa Lyman to retrieve the tithing that Sam Brannon was supposed to have collected on behalf of the Church.

Sam Brannon was an early convert to the Church in the days when it was still centered in Kirtland, Ohio. He moved to New York City where he started a Latter-day Saint newspaper. After the exodus to Utah began, Brannon persuaded Brigham Young to let him bring a group of Saints to Utah via California on the ship *Brooklyn*. When the ship arrived in Yerba Buena, soon to be renamed San Francisco, the 240 Mormons who landed tripled the size of San Francisco. Brannon made his way across California, Nevada, and Utah to meet with Brigham Young on

---

41 Jerry Borrowman Note: This group of the Mormon Battalion included my great-great grandfather, John Borrowman. A convert from Canada, John Borrowman was also an early pioneer who ultimately settled in Nephi, Utah, giving up his inheritance in Canada in order to join the Church. For a full account of John Borrowman's experience as an early pioneer, please see "A Halfpenny and a Pearl," *Ensign*, September 1996, 23.

the Mormon Trail in an attempt to persuade him to make the main settlement of the Church in Northern California, where the climate was hospitable, the land was fertile and easy to till, and transportation was accessible by ship to San Francisco and up the American River as far as Sacramento. But Brigham Young did not want to settle in a place where other emigrants wanted to go, judging that the old resentments that had led to their persecution in Ohio, Missouri, and Illinois would simply be repeated. Brannon returned to California disappointed, but he wasn't entirely empty-handed since Brigham Young had authorized him to collect tithes from the passengers on the *Brooklyn*.

Apparently he did this and then misused the money as a personal resource to buy up every shovel in Northern California in anticipation of the coming gold rush. Returning to San Francisco, he went up and down the streets shouting, "Gold, gold, gold from the American River." Having locked up most of the implements and dry goods needed to outfit the miners using tithing funds, he was well positioned to make a fortune from the sale of supplies to the would-be millionaires who now flooded into California.

When Porter and Elder Lyman met up with Brannon in California, they requested the tithing which he had been entrusted with. Brannon was reported to say, "Show me a receipt signed by God and I'll give you the tithing." Had Elder Lyman been able to produce such a receipt, he would have had to dismantle Samuel Brannon's new mansion brick by brick, since that's where the profits from the tithing money investment had been spent. Brannon was eventually disfellowshipped from the Church for encouraging vigilante activities in San Francisco. He went on to earn and lose a number of fortunes and stands out a colorful character in the history of the Church.

With their primary mission frustrated, Elder Lyman released Porter so he could go to work in the gold fields, panning for gold. He tried this for a while but eventually concluded that he wasn't going to get rich wading knee-deep in the gold-rich American River. Even though men could earn up to $60 per day at a time when a laborer in San Francisco was lucky to get 60 cents per day, the cost of living being charged the miners was commensurate with their income. That was the kind of math Porter Rockwell understood, and he decided that the best way to get rich was panning miners. So he opened the Round Tent Saloon on Murderer's Bar in the American River. He opened two small hotels out in the gold fields as well. His businesses were an instant success, particularly since he developed a very innovative way to let the miners know when he was returning by wagon from San Francisco with a new load of whiskey. As he arrived near the mouth of the canyon where the saloon was located, he would take out a bugle and blow a tune (showing that he had some musical ability), which would echo up and down the canyon walls, letting the miners know that there was fresh whiskey at the Round Tent Saloon.

Porter seemed to relish life in California, especially enjoying the various shooting contests that were popular in California at that time. Porter always won, which annoyed people, but it also gave them a healthy respect for Porter that helped him maintain order at his saloons.[42]

Even after leaving Missouri, Porter sometimes went by the alias James Brown to keep out of trouble. One day Porter competed in a contest with a man, beating him quite handily. The fellow was sullen about this but became considerably more animated as he started drinking his way through some of Porter's whiskey at the Round Tent. When he was fully inebriated, he started shooting his mouth off by telling everyone who "Mr. Brown" really was—the infamous Porter Rockwell. This was dangerous for Porter because Governor Boggs himself was living in California at this time. Boggs still maintained that Porter had

---

42 Jean Baptiste Charbonneau, son of Sacagawea, frequented Rockwell's Round Tent Saloon. It is possible the two met.

shot him, so Porter decided it was time for him to pack up all the gold he'd collected from the miners and make his way back to Utah. He went out into the gold fields and called on some of the Mormon miners who were there and convinced them to join him in his journey to Salt Lake, bringing all their gold as well. The remarkable part is that Porter and these brothers in the gospel committed to give all of their gold to Brigham Young, which they did as soon as they'd made the arduous crossing of the Sierra-Nevada Mountains and across the Nevada and northern Utah desert to Salt Lake City. Brigham Young was grateful, since the demands on the Church treasury were endless.

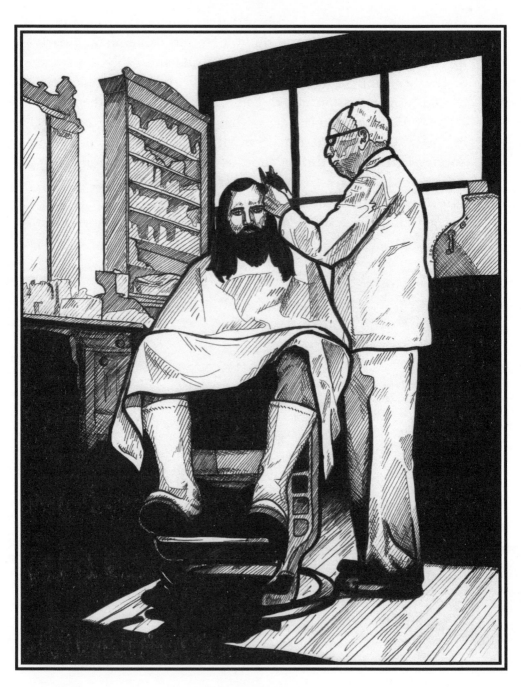

PORTER CUTS HIS HAIR

IN AUGUST 1854, COLONEL EDWARD Jenner Steptoe led three hundred soldiers into Salt Lake City, where he was to serve as the military governor of the Utah Territory. Brigham Young was the civilian governor. Steptoe was offered Brigham Young's position in December 1854, but he declined and recommended to the U.S. president that Brigham Young be reappointed, which is what happened.

Steptoe then had the freedom to complete a number of other assignments he'd been given, including investigating the so-called Gunnison Massacre at the hands of the Paiute Indians. In a convoluted line of reasoning, the Mormons were blamed for this massacre in which Captain John W. Gunnison and seven men in his surveying expedition for the Pacific Railroad were attacked and killed by the Paiute Indians. The Paiutes killed this group in retaliation for an earlier attack on the Indians by a wagon train of Missouri immigrants who had killed two of the Paiutes. It was widely assumed in the East that the infamous Porter Rockwell must have had something to do with it.

Oddly enough, Colonel Steptoe hired Porter and two other Mormons, George Bean and Nicholas Janise, to negotiate with the Paiutes for the surrender of the guilty braves. The Paiute chief had no intention of turning over the guilty braves, because young men were too valuable to the survival of the tribe, but he did agree to surrender eight Indians, who were then taken to Salt Lake City in a military wagon. The decrepit group he turned over to the Army included one woman, one blind man, one mentally impaired man, one sick and elderly man, and one outsider who was not a Paiute, as well as three young boys. Steptoe knew he'd been outwitted by the chief, but he had to accept the situation.

Steptoe's other assignment was to find a better route from Salt Lake City to Carson Valley, California. He had already sent two men to scout the route, but when it was time to lead his soldiers west, Porter Rockwell was hired to guide the troops. Rockwell urged the captain to also hire his young friend George W. Bean. Rockwell's knowledge of the west desert and the fact that he'd been to California twice before were invaluable to the success of the journey. At the end of the expedition, Colonel Steptoe wrote a letter of recommendation for Rockwell, giving him credit for the success of getting his troops safely to California.

Now that he was back in California, Porter decided to visit his old haunts of the gold rush days. He also visited his sister Electa in California and spent time at a hotel on the shores of the Pacific Ocean. While there he happened to meet Agnes Smith, the widow of Don Carlos Smith, the younger brother of Joseph Smith. Agnes had just recovered from a severe bout of typhoid fever, which caused all of her hair to fall out, and she was very embarrassed by her appearance. To this point in time, Porter had never cut his hair or his beard since receiving the blessing of safety at the hands of Joseph Smith in Nauvoo. But as a gesture of kindness to Agnes and out of love for the Smith family, Porter secretly went to a barber, had his hair cut, took the long braids to a wig maker and had a wig made for Agnes.

Agnes was extremely grateful, appreciating how much it cost Porter to cut his hair in light of Joseph Smith's promise.

Afterward, Porter went into hiding, claiming that he wasn't going to face the outlaws of the West without his hair to protect him.

He also said jokingly that after having his hair cut, he could no longer control his desire for strong drink and cussing. As his hair started to grow out again, Porter finally started the long and arduous trek back to Utah. But with all the skills he'd gained in his previous experience in the wilderness, he was able to make this trip in just thirteen days—an astounding accomplishment. That was less than half the time it had taken any other individual or group to cross the west desert on their way to Salt Lake City.[43]

---

43 The story of Rockwell cutting his hair was told by Elizebeth Roundy in her letter to the Church. The story also appeared in the "Church Section" of the *Deseret News,* August 31, 1835.

THE UTAH MORMON WAR

TEN YEARS AFTER ARRIVING IN Salt Lake City, relations between the Mormons in Utah and the United States government were in shambles. When the Saints first arrived in the valley in 1847, Utah was not even part of the United States. That changed with America's victory in the Mexican-American War—a victory aided by the service of the Mormon Battalion. After annexation, Brigham Young had been appointed governor of Utah, which allowed the Saints to prosper and grow in their remote mountain valleys with very little outside control or conflict.

But by 1857, President James Buchanan was under intense public pressure to name a non-Mormon governor to replace Brigham Young. There were a number of reasons that public sentiment was hostile toward the Mormons, chief of which was the practice of polygamy. Not only did the vast majority of Americans consider this immoral, but it was often tied in the press to the practice of slavery. Politicians in the Southern states who argued that slavery was a matter of states' rights recognized that the same argument would logically extend to the practice of polygamy. Thus you had one practice that virtually everyone outside of the Church felt was immoral—polygamy—that was confusing the debate about whether to allow states to choose another practice that only part of the country condemned as immoral—slavery. Politicians on both ends of the political spectrum were hostile to the Mormons because of this linkage in the public mind.

The Civil War was still four years in the future, but the political pressure was building to a boiling point. As antagonism toward the Mormons increased, President Buchanan saw political opportunity to deflect attention away from slavery and focus it on the Saints.

Other reasons that the public was hostile to the Saints included a sense that Brigham Young had created a theocracy in the West that ran counter to the democratic ideal of American politics. Even though the Mormons celebrated the Fourth of July and declared their loyalty to the United States, Church leaders often held both religious and secular leadership positions in the same community. For example, in many communities the bishop was also the mayor. This unified leadership gave Brigham Young an unusual amount of power. The notion of a Mormon dictatorship was reinforced by reports sent back to Washington by the non-Mormon officials living in Utah who declared that the Saints were hostile and threatening to them to the point that many started resigning their posts out of "fear for their lives."

Inasmuch as Buchanan wanted to avoid making any decisions about slavery, the chance to send an army to Utah to suppress the universally despised Mormons seemed like a political opportunity that he could not pass up. So the president was persuaded that a rebellion was imminent in Utah. He appointed Alfred Cumming as the new territorial governor but failed to notify Brigham Young that he was being replaced. He also ordered the creation of an army, approximately 2,500 in number, to accompany the new governor to Utah to help him enforce the laws when requested by civil authorities. Again, no notice of this was given to Brigham Young, which would lead the Saints to conclude the worst possible motives.

The way that this plan was discovered in Utah involved Porter Rockwell. Porter carried the U.S. mail from Salt Lake City to Fort Laramie, Wyoming. While out on the trail, he encountered Abraham O. Smoot and Judson Stoddard coming from the East with news that the U.S. Army had been deployed to put down a supposed rebellion in Utah and was assembling at Fort Leavenworth, Kansas, to begin their march west.

Porter, Smoot, and Stoddard left Fort Laramie in a light spring wagon to take the news to Brigham, with Porter at the reins. They covered the 512 miles in just five days and three hours. Arriving in Salt Lake City, they found the city empty because everyone was up Big Cottonwood Canyon celebrating the Fourth of July and their first ten years in Utah. Porter and the others came riding into the camp to brief Brigham Young on the news of the army. Brigham Young reacted swiftly, telling the Saints of the unhappy news. In the days that followed, he put the Nauvoo Legion on alert and told the Saints to prepare themselves for the possibility of abandoning Salt Lake City. Almost immediately he started developing plans to harass the army as it made its way to Utah, and he would eventually declare martial law in order to control the various emigrant parties that passed through Utah on their way to California and Oregon. The Saints had been driven out of their homes three times before this, and they weren't going to let it happen again without a fight.

Brigham Young was largely successful in his strategies. By the time Johnston's army arrived a year later, after having suffered terribly in Wyoming because of the successful Mormon raids on their supply trains, they would find the houses in Salt Lake stuffed with straw so that the Mormons could burn the city to the ground rather than allow it to be occupied by a "foreign" army. The Utah Mormon War comprised one full year of diligent preparation by the Saints, who felt they were being harassed and oppressed for their religious beliefs. It also became a frustrating year for the appointed officials who were supposed to replace Brigham Young's administration and for the army escorting them as they were challenged on the open plains of Wyoming. Porter Rockwell would play a vital role in these sorties.

After receiving much harassment, the army arrived in Salt Lake City on June 26, 1858. General Johnston, angry about the harassment of his troops by men like Porter, would be heard to say as he rode through the empty streets of Salt Lake City that he would have given "his plantation for a chance to bombard the city for fifteen minutes," while his assistant, Lieutenant Colonel Charles F. Smith stated even more bluntly with interspersed cursing that he "did not care . . . who heard him; he would like to see every . . . Mormon hung [*sic*] by the neck."[44]

There were many among the Saints who wanted to go to war with the army. Brigham Young kept a level head, however, and managed, with the help of an old friend to the Mormons, to avoid bloodshed. Colonel Thomas Kane was sent to negotiate a peace between the army and the Saints. Brigham Young was no longer governor, but he managed to retain a much greater degree of latitude than the federal government originally intended. When the conflict was over, public sentiment in the East would call it "Buchanan's Blunder," with the president falling under severe censure for having failed to first investigate the exaggerated claims of the complainers before mustering an army or to even open a dialogue with Brigham Young. In speaking of the Utah Mormon War, a reporter for the *New York Herald* wrote, "Thus was peace made—thus was ended the 'Mormon war,' which . . . may be thus historisized: Killed, none; wounded, none; fooled, everybody."[45]

The eventual outcome of the war was that Johnston's army was allowed to enter a deserted Salt Lake City. Passing through, they set up a headquarters at Camp Floyd to the southwest of Salt Lake City, on the western side of Utah Lake, where they weren't seen as a menace. The Saints moved back into Salt Lake, and life started to return to normal, although many farmers missed out on an entire season of planting crops, business owners suffering financial losses and other everyday interruptions. Eventually, Camp Floyd would be abandoned

44 Donald L. Moormon and Gene A. Sessions. *Camp Floyd and the Mormons: the Utah War,* 49.

45 William P. McKinnon. *Causes of the Utah War.* (Fort Douglas Vedette, 2007).

when the Civil War broke out, with federal property sold at a steep discount to the local Mormons. In time, the army would establish another outpost at Fort Douglas on the western foothills of the Wasatch Mountains, as much to protect against Indians as to keep a watchful eye on the Mormons.

HARASSING JOHNSTON'S ARMY

You should "[ascertain] the locality or route of the troops [and] proceed at once to annoy them in every possible way. Use every exertion to stampede their animals, and set fire to their trains. Burn the whole country before them and on their flanks. . . . Take no life, but destroy their trains, and stampede or drive away their animals, at every opportunity."[46]

—Brigham Young

ONCE BRIGHAM YOUNG HAD DECIDED on a course of action, he asked Porter and others in the militia to travel to Wyoming to slow the advance of the army. The army was traveling without cavalry, making the job easier. The infantry was marching across the desert with supply wagons and horses to assist in the effort. It was relatively easy for the Mormons to sneak up on a camp at night and untie the horses before the soldiers could respond.

The first real encounter between the Mormons and the army occurred in late September 1847, when the militia came upon the army slowly making its way through Wyoming near South Pass. The first thing they did was to torch the grass along the trail and stampede the army's cattle. The Mormons then made their way to Fort Bridger to burn it to the ground so the advancing army could not take refuge there in the winter.

---

46 Brigham Young, as quoted by Leonard J. Arrington. *Brigham Young: American Moses*, 255.

A few days later, the Mormons managed to burn three large supply trains that were caught out in the open, confiscating a large number of cattle and horses that they took west with them to help supply the militia's needs during the forthcoming battles and through the long winter. The army would suffer hunger and deprivation because of these raids.

On one occasion the army got the better of Porter when he attempted to steal some army mules. His mistake was in not tying up the Mormons' own horses well enough. Sneaking up on the army camp, he went in and liberated a small herd of their mules—very hardy animals that were excellent for packing but almost as stubbornly independent as Porter himself. As he successfully led the mules and his own horses away from the camp, he'd reached the point where he should have been in the clear. He dismounted to rest his horses. Unfortunately for Porter, the army sergeant in charge of the mules knew enough about the animals to blow the bugle. The mules were trained that when the bugle sounded they were going to be fed. Just as soon as the mules heard the bugle, they immediately turned around and headed back to camp. As animals will do, Porter's horses followed the mules. That left Porter and his men on foot until they met up with some others from the Nauvoo Legion who provided them with new mounts. Eventually, Porter was able to steal his horses back again, but it made for some interesting drama.

Porter became so skilled at sneaking up on the military camps that he could often hear their conversations, which provided him with military intelligence. He also got to hear their frustrated gossip about Porter's and the Nauvoo Legion's exploits.

The winter of 1847–48 was very cold, particularly for those members of the Nauvoo Legion who were stuck out on the barren Wyoming plains doing their best to aggravate the army. But their efforts were successful in giving Brigham Young time to prepare the Salt Lake valley before the spring weather reopened the trail in 1848.

Probably the cleverest ruse of the Utah Mormon War occurred when the new federally appointed governor, Alfred Cumming, decided that he would accept Brigham Young's invitation to come into Salt Lake City with a handful of military officers, but under Brigham Young's personal protection, to attempt to negotiate a peaceful settlement.

To get to Salt Lake City, the governor and his party had to pass through Echo Canyon to the east of the Salt Lake valley. In doing so, they were to be treated to an elaborate charade that would cause the governor to vastly overestimate the strength of Mormon resistance if the military were to try to force their way into the valley. It simply isn't recorded whether the idea for this guile belonged to Porter, but he certainly played his part in the deception very well.

As Governor Cumming reached the summit of the pass, he was invited to a cordial dinner with leaders of the Nauvoo Legion who were under the command of Elder Daniel H. Wells of the First Presidency and Colonel Robert T. Burton. It was night by the time the governor's party was allowed to enter the canyon, with Porter at the reins of the governor's carriage. Almost immediately they were stopped by sentries, who forced them to alight from their carriages to be inspected and their identification papers checked. While all this was happening, other members of the legion scurried ahead on the trail and took up position high on the canyon walls. Once released from the sentry, the carriage proceeded slowly down the trail under Porter's able control. While passing under the cliffs, the men in the carriage could see campfires high on the canyon walls, hear the whistled or shouted recognition signals, and listen to the sound of rustling in the underbrush that sounded like troops moving into position.

But as soon as the party passed a given location, the fires would quickly be extinguished, and the men would race down the canyon to a lower spot where they would light new fires. To give them time to take up position, Porter's carriage would be stopped by another group of "sentries" who would patiently ask the party to descend, check their papers, etc. And then they'd move on to be surrounded by new fires and new troops calling out their recognition symbols, even though it was the same men they had encountered earlier.

By the time the party made its way into Salt Lake City later that night, Governor Cumming was convinced that a massive contingent of thousands of Mormons was lining the canyon walls to defend the city. In truth, there were no more than 150 Nauvoo legionnaires involved in the whole enterprise.

After meeting with Brigham Young, peace negotiations were settled, and the army agreed that they would not establish their military post any closer than forty miles from Salt Lake City. When the army finally arrived in Salt Lake City that next summer, it was allowed to march right down Main Street. Colonel Thomas L. Kane, a personal friend of Brigham Young who was instrumental in the negotiations, marched with them down the street bareheaded as a sign of respect for the Saints.

Just in case the military decided to renege on their promise not to occupy Salt Lake City, Brigham Young had ordered all the houses to be filled with straw, with enough men left behind to light them on fire if Brigham gave the signal. This aggravated General Johnston, but it also showed him just how resolved the Mormons were to not fall under military rule.

Fortunately the military lived up to its commitment and went to Camp Floyd to the southwest of the city.

After his long absence from home, Porter was now free to see to the needs of his family along with all the other Saints who had abandoned Salt Lake City in anticipation of the possible siege. He now moved his family out of Utah Valley and back to their original home in the Salt Lake valley. The Utah Mormon War was over.

THE AIKEN BROTHERS

In 1857, AT THE HEIGHT of tensions between the Mormons and Johnston's army, a group of six gamblers, including John and Tom Aiken, packed up their gambling outfit and gear in California with the intent to find Johnston's army on the western plains. Their goal was simple—to fleece the soldiers out of their earnings. These well-seasoned gamblers of the gold rush days joined a Mormon wagon train in Carson Valley headed for Utah. Beyond picking the soldiers' pockets, they also intended to set up a gambling house, saloon, and a house of prostitution in the heart of Zion, with the soldiers their prime customers.

Arriving in Utah before striking out for Johnston's army in Wyoming, the group of rogues became suspicious to the Mormons in the area because of all their talk about joining up with the army, so they were eventually arrested as spies. It would have been ludicrous for Brigham Young to allow them to reach the army out in Wyoming. Even if they were not spies, at this point they knew far too much about the preparations being made in Salt Lake City and other towns in Utah in advance of Johnston's army, and it was clear they'd be willing to divulge this to the military for a price. After holding them for a time, Church leaders finally decided to escort four of the men out of Utah territory but not to the east. The two others were released and left the territory on their own.

In Lehi, the four remaining men were turned over to Porter Rockwell and Sylvanus Collett, who were joined by two or three other men as the escort party. They were going to take the men south to Nevada and, presumably, back to California. The party passed through Nephi and finally camped on the Sevier River.

Allegedly, two of the Californians were killed out in the wilderness along the Sevier River and the other two escaped, showing up in Nephi a few days later, bloodied and desperate. They were also killed a short time later while making their way to Salt Lake City. The circumstances of all these deaths were unclear.

When word of all this reached the more populous areas of the state, Gentile newspapers at first printed that the party was attacked by Indians, something common in this region. Later, however, these same newspapers would change their story and accuse the Mormons of murdering the Aiken party, which was a direct accusation against Porter.

Anti-Mormon prejudice fueled the flames of the wildest rumors, and eventually blame for the "assassinations" was laid at the feet of Brigham Young, who, it was said, ordered the killings in order to rob the Aiken party of their $25,000 worth of gold. In truth, the men had only $4,000 worth of gold—still a sizeable sum—but with each telling of the story the gold miraculously grew like loaves of bread and fishes, to $8,000, $12,000, $18,000, and finally $25,000.

The story eventually died down, with little attention paid to it. There is no record that Porter ever discussed what happened to the Aiken party, and no charges were brought against Porter or other members of the escort at the time it happened.

The continuation of this story picked up twenty years later, in 1877. With the successful arrest, conviction, and execution of John D. Lee for his involvement and leadership in the infamous Mountain Meadow Massacre near Cedar City, the federal authorities in Salt Lake decided to reopen the Aiken case. Having won a victory against the Mormons in the Lee case, they felt they could bring up other charges to discredit the leaders of the Church, even a case that was now twenty years old. These weren't the only charges brought against prominent Mormons. Even Brigham Young had been arrested on counterfeiting charges, which required Porter and three of his friends to put up $25,000 in bonds to get Brigham out of jail. It was a dark time for Church leadership, with the fragile peace that was negotiated at the end of the Utah Mormon War being challenged by hostile federal officials once again.

In 1877, an arrest warrant was issued against Rockwell, Brigham Young, and others for the alleged Aiken killings. Porter spent six days in jail before being allowed bail. Three of his friends put up $15,000. He hired two attorneys to defend him, but they had a very difficult time getting their client to help with his own defense. When questioned about what had happened twenty years earlier, Rockwell would only reply, "All is wheat, all is wheat," a phrase that meant "all is fine." Apparently Porter had confidence that he would be exonerated.

But 1877 was also the year that Brigham Young died, and Porter died not long afterward, in 1878. Both were gone before the trial was held, and so their version of the story went to the grave with them. Yet a trial was held in October 1878, with Sylvanus Collett as the defendant. He was charged, along with Porter, for murdering the Aikens twenty years earlier. The course and outcome of this trial is very important to Porter Rockwell's history, since the Aiken trial has hung over Porter's reputation for more than a century.

During the trial, the prosecution failed to prove that any murders had been committed, while the defense was able to establish that all the evidence against Collett and against Rockwell was hearsay or circumstantial evidence. Witnesses for the prosecution gave contradictory testimony, some of which suggested Brigham Young's orders and overheard expressions of a "botched job," but their claims were easily ripped apart by Collett's attorneys. In the end, the jury found Collett not guilty. While Porter could not be found either guilty or innocent after his death, Collett's acquittal would certainly have been the outcome for Porter's trial, had it been held.

So what did happen in 1857? Was the party actually attacked by Indians? Recent research suggests that it is possible. Another possibility is that the Aiken party attempted an escape and were killed in the attempt. Porter had not disarmed them, because they were only being escorted out of the state to protect military intelligence. Records show that they were armed quite heavily, with twenty-four pistols and plenty of ammunition. An argument could have broken out around the campfire along the trail on the Sevier River, followed by the men's attempt to break free and an ensuing gunfight. We can only speculate.

There is an interesting branch to this story. Sometime after the Aiken incident, a man named Joachim Johnston hired some outlaws to steal some mules from a non-Mormon freighter who'd been hired by the military. Joachim was angry at the military for breaking up his place at Camp Floyd. When Porter and his posse finally caught up with Joachim Johnston in Las Vegas, then a small watering station on the way to California, Joachim admitted his guilt, telling Porter, "I didn't think you'd come after me for stealing from your enemies." But Porter was a duly appointed lawman, and this shows that he administered justice impartially.

Joachim Johnston was guilty of a capital offense, but he bargained for his release, telling Porter that he could take the mules back to the military in Salt Lake if he would allow Johnston to continue on his way to California. Strangely enough, Porter agreed, and Porter and his posse, now comprising the four other Mormons that Johnston had hired to herd the mules for him, left the mules to winter along the Santa Clara River near St. George, and Johnston went on his way, a free man. The following spring, Porter returned to pick up the mules and herded them back to Salt Lake.

What makes this story significant, particularly in view of the accusations leveled at Porter in the Aiken deaths, is that while Porter was often accused of being judge, jury, and executioner (and in spite of his claims that if he ever chased an outlaw more than a hundred miles, he wouldn't bring him back alive), he did allow Joachim Johnston to go free and returned the others in the party to testify against the original thieves.

The true story of the Aiken party is likely to remain shrouded and a continuing source of controversy, but the only man to stand trial was acquitted by a jury.

PORTER AND THE OUTLAWS

Porter Rockwell—
Territorial Deputy Marshal

PORTER AT CAMP FLOYD

WHILE JOHNSTON'S ARMY WAS SEQUESTERED at Camp Floyd in the west desert, Porter had occasion to go out there on some business. But on the night before he arrived, one of the local houses of entertainment had burned down, and the soldiers at Camp Floyd blamed Porter.

When Porter rode into camp the next day like nothing had happened, the men were outraged because they were frustrated at losing their female companionship. Soon Porter found himself surrounded by soldiers who were threatening to kill him.

In classic Porter Rockwell style, he pulled out two Colt pistols faster than an eye could follow his hands, dropped his reins on the horn of his saddle, spurred his horse into a widening circle to get the men away from him while calling out, "If any of you lay hands on me, you will not leave Utah alive!" Even though he was far outnumbered, the soldiers backed off and let him enter the fort. Porter went to the officers' quarters, tied his horse to the hitching rail, and conducted his business inside. When finished, he came out and very calmly mounted his horse and rode off unharmed.

It's something of a mystery how he could do things like that, but he did.

THE CASE OF THE GREAT BULLION ROBBERY

AT TIMES, PORTER WAS HIRED by Wells Fargo to ride as a special agent to protect their stage coach lines. When doing so he would often ride "shotgun." This was especially the case when gold shipments were involved, since Wells Fargo trusted Porter's honesty and his ability to deal with outlaws. They also knew that the Indians would leave the stage coach alone when they saw Porter riding as shotgun; the Indians knew about Porter's hair and the promise given him that he could not be killed, and they believed the prophecy.

On one such occasion, Porter was waiting for the stage to arrive at Faust Station in the west desert. As the stage came down the hill at Lookout Pass toward Faust Station, Porter noticed something was wrong—the stage was coming in way too fast. When the coach finally arrived at Faust Station, the driver excitedly told Porter what had happened, explaining that as the coach rounded a bend at Riverbed in the west desert, a man was lying dead in the middle of the trail. The driver stopped the stage coach and stepped down to check on the dead man. He used the toe of his boot to turn the dead man over, only to see the man come instantly to his feet with a gun in hand, pointing it in the face of the driver. The robber quickly took the $40,000 in gold that was being transported in the strongbox and dragged it to the side of the road where he had a horse hidden in the trees, and off he disappeared. The stagecoach driver then drove as fast as he could from Riverbed to Faust Station.

Porter accepted responsibility for bringing the thief to justice, supplied himself with cold rations, and then set off alone to Riverbed. There he found where the stagecoach had been robbed. Porter followed the robber's trail to the south and east to an area called Cherry Creek. From his vantage point up in the hills, he noticed a man making camp along the river's edge. For several days, Porter kept his eye on him through his spyglass. Finally, after breakfast one morning, the man took his shovel in hand and went off into the cedar trees. As he was pulling out the last bar of gold bullion, Porter shoved a pistol in his back, arrested him, and took the robber and the gold to his ranch at Government Creek.

Arriving late in the evening, Porter told his foreman, Hat Shirtliff, to guard the man while Porter got some needed sleep. He had been awake for many days and nights waiting to see what the outlaw would do and where he had the gold hidden.

During the night, the foreman dozed off, and the robber made a quick escape and got onto a horse. In the commotion of his escape, Porter awoke. Sensing what had happened, he ran to the door of the ranch house with pistol in hand and fired a shot into the dark. The gunshot was followed immediately by a scream. Lighting a lantern, Porter and Shirtliff looked for the man, but they couldn't find him. The outlaw had made his escape.

A few days later, Porter was in Salt Lake City, turning all of the retrieved gold over to Wells Fargo and explaining what had happened to the robber.

About a week later, a telegraph arrived in Salt Lake City from the Fort Bridger area. It was the outlaw claiming that Porter had robbed the outlaw of the gold and kept it for himself. However, a short time after that, riders coming along the telegraph line into Salt Lake City discovered a dead man with a makeshift telegraph key in his hand and a large bullet hole in his side. Porter had brought the robber to justice, after all.

THE BEAR RIVER MASSACRE

WHEN THE SHOSHONE INDIANS WERE harassing the wagon trains in southern Idaho near Preston, Colonel Connor was instructed to suppress the Indians with force, if necessary, to protect the wagon trains and mail routes. The Indians were angry that the animals on the emigrant trains were eating all the grass, and the whites in the area were upset because of increasingly brutal Indian raids. Antagonism between the Indians and the whites had built to a breaking point.

Colonel Connor solicited the help of Porter to be his scout in the event that came to be called the Bear River Massacre. In his role as scout, Porter led the military through the January snowdrifts down into the river valley where the Indians were encamped. When the army arrived, they found the Indians entrenched with breastworks, rifle ports, and a series of trenches from which to fight. They were ready and anxious for battle. Negotiations between the army and the Indians broke down very quickly, and shots were fired. For the next few hours, a furious battle ensued. It's most likely that Porter participated in the battle, but as it became apparent that the engagement would be far more deadly than anticipated, Porter left and went to the nearby Mormon settlements to ask for sleighs and wagons to bring to the battlefield to retrieve the wounded soldiers.

As the day wore on and the army soldiers gained the advantage, they slew many of the male Indians, and then in a battle-crazed frenzy they turned on the Indian women and children. It was a gruesome affair that went way beyond what was needed. But the idea of a battle to suppress the Indians and bring order to the territory had been encouraged even by the editorial writers of the *Deseret News* who had written,

> With ordinary good luck, the volunteers will "wipe them out." We wish this community rid of all such parties, and if Col. Connor be successful in reaching that . . . class of humans who play with the lives of the peaceable and law abiding citizens in this way, we shall be pleased to acknowledge our obligations.[47]

These were hard times and good people called for harsh measures to find peace and safety.

While Porter's exact role in the attack is not well documented, it is known that Colonel Connor wrote in official

---

47 Brigham D. Madsen. *Glory Hunter: A Biography of Patrick Edward Connor.* (Salt Lake City, Utah: University of Utah Press, 1990), 79.

military records that he believed Porter Rockwell was responsible for saving most of his men's lives. Colonel Connor was very anti-Mormon, but Porter and Colonel Connor became good friends through Porter's service to the army.

THE CHAUNCEY MILLARD INCIDENT

ROCKWELL WAS OFTEN ACCUSED DURING his lifetime of being judge, jury, and executioner, who seldom brought his prisoners in alive when acting in the role of a deputy marshal for the territory of Utah. The Chauncey Millard case is yet another incident that proves otherwise.

The Nevada White Pine County silver mines were in need of supplies. A Salt Lake City freighter by the name of Champion Mayfield saw in this a financial opportunity, so he loaded three wagons with potatoes and onions and hired two men to help him drive the wagons into Nevada. The two men were Harlan P. Swett and an eighteen-year-old drifter from New York named Chauncey Millard. The three men left Salt Lake City on December 8, 1868. A few days later, they stopped at the base of Rattle Snake Bluff on the west shore of Utah Lake to prepare lunch. Swett prepared the meal over a campfire. In the meantime, Mayfield was going through his belongings and noticed his revolver was missing. He turned to ask Swett if he had the weapon, but just as he did so, he heard a shot, and Swett yelled out, "I'm shot!" Turning, Mayfield saw the man fall to the ground. Chauncey Millard was standing over him with the gun in his hand.

Mayfield yelled at Millard, who now turned the gun on him and began to empty the revolver. Though wounded in the hand, Mayfield ran for his life, throwing off his coat as he ran. After Mayfield was out of sight, Chauncey Millard rummaged through the wagons, looking for the $600 in gold coins that he knew Mayfield was carrying. Not finding the gold, Millard thought it best to escape. He didn't know that the gold was in the coat that his boss had just discarded a few yards from the camp. Millard tried to mount one of the horses in the outfit, but it threw him to the ground, so he made his escape on foot.

After watching this from a hiding place, Mayfield made his way to a farmhouse and was taken into Lehi, where a local doctor treated his wounded hand. A Lehi posse was formed to go out and bring the young killer in, but it failed to find him. They did, however, find Swett's frozen body and returned it to Lehi.

Soon after this incident, a man named John Irvin arrived in Lehi to report that his camp in Cedar Valley had been looted by a young man who had been at his camp and that his shotgun and ammunition were missing. The next day, a teamster came into Lehi and reported that he had noticed a young man along the road west of Fairfield.

At this point the Lehi authorities knew it was time to call in a professional. A telegram was sent into Salt Lake City for help. Soon thereafter, Territorial Marshal Orrin Porter Rockwell and fellow officer Henry Heath arrived in Lehi and gathered all the information they needed before heading out on the manhunt.

About sunrise on December 17, the marshals rode up to a sheep camp in Rush Valley where they spotted young Chauncey Millard. Rockwell ordered Millard to surrender, and the young man wisely chose not to resist. By sundown that same day, Chauncey Millard was locked up in the jail located in the basement of the tithing house in Lehi. The next morning, the prisoner was taken by Rockwell into Provo for trial, where Millard was found guilty of the crime. He was executed on January 29, 1869.

In something of a macabre act of defiance before his execution, Millard sold the rights to his body to a local physician by the name of Roberts in exchange for a pound of candy, which Millard calmly ate just before he was taken to the firing squad.[48]

---

48 For references, see *Deseret News* articles beginning the December 18, 1868, and ending on the February 10, 1869.

This incident shows that Porter did his best to bring his prisoners in alive to face justice of the court, as long as they cooperated.

PORTER AND THE HORSE THIEVES

LOT HUNTINGTON

JOHN BENNION, A PROMINENT MORMON and friend of Rockwell, lived in Taylorsville, southwest of Salt Lake City. One evening he rode his favorite horse, a thoroughbred named Brown Sal, to tithing settlement at his bishop's home. When he came out, the horse was gone. Bennion quickly walked home, told his son Sam what had happened, and Sam and a few friends started searching for the horse while another person was sent to get Rockwell. That same night, Rockwell, Bennion, his son Sam, and two others set out to find the horse.

When they arrived at Camp Floyd, they were told that a young outlaw by the name of Lot Huntington and two others had been there earlier with Bennion's horse. So the party continued traveling, even though it was very late at night. Arriving at Faust Station at 4:00 AM, Porter positioned his men around the bunkhouse while Porter stood behind the woodpile, waiting for sunup. The outlaws were in the bunkhouse having breakfast when Doc Faust, who owned the station, came out of the bunkhouse to throw out the dishwater. Porter got his attention and told him to go back inside and "tell those boys in there that they're arrested for being horse thieves." Faust agreed and went inside. Two of the gang came out with their hands up—they were not going to try to face down Porter Rockwell. But Lot Huntington was a tough guy. He came out with pistol in hand, threatening to kill Porter if he didn't let Huntington get away free and clear.

"Lot, don't make me kill you," said Porter. But Huntington was not dissuaded and started to make his way to the stable, where he maneuvered to keep his horse between himself and Porter while putting on the saddle. All the while, Huntington was holding his gun over the horse's back so he could shoot Porter if he tried anything.

As Hungtington was leading the horse out of the corral, it bumped its nose on the rails of the corral and the horse reared. In the brief instant that the horse reared up, leaving Huntington partially exposed, Porter fired a single round, and Lot Huntington fell backward over the rails of the corral with a bullet in his heart.

Porter put his body in a wagon, and they took it back to Salt Lake, along with the other two horse thieves, who were turned over to the local police officers. Later, the two thieves made the mistake of trying to escape, perhaps thinking they stood a better chance when it wasn't Porter behind the gun, but the local police officers shot and killed them both.

STOLEN MULES AND HORSES

IN 1861, FRANK KARRICK HAD a profitable business hauling freight between Sacramento and Salt Lake City. He was camped seventy miles south of Salt Lake City when Karrick discovered nine of his animals missing. They were valued at more than $4,000. He ordered his teamsters to mind the camp while he rode off to find his mules and a valuable stallion that was also missing. But he lost the trail forty miles from the camp. Arriving back at his camp, he secretly buried $15,000 in gold coin that he had in his wagon, perhaps not trusting his men to guard it for him. Then he rode off for Salt Lake City, where he sought help from Brigham Young. Even though Brigham was no longer territorial governor, he was still the man to see when you needed something done. Brigham told Karrick to seek the services of Rockwell. Later that same day, Porter and Karrick were in the saddle, heading south. Karrick took Porter to the spot where he had lost the trail. Porter got down and studied the place for a few minutes, quickly remounted his horse, and sped off with Karrick doing his best to keep up. By sunset of the next day, Rockwell had caught up with the rustlers. Sneaking up on their camp, Porter and Karrick found the two outlaws sitting around a campfire. With his Colt revolver in hand, Rockwell surprised the men and ordered them to throw their hands in the air. Wisely, they complied. Rockwell, Karrick, and the two rustlers then herded the animals to the nearest Mormon settlement, where Rockwell turned his prisoners over to the local sheriff. Porter didn't always shoot first and ask questions later.

Arriving at Karrick's camp later that evening, Karrick dug up his gold and counted out $500 and handed it to Rockwell. Porter looked at the money, a very large amount for a few days' work, and said, "Son, you'd better keep it. I have more of that than you do." But Karrick insisted. The two said good-bye, and Rockwell headed home. Several weeks later, two packages arrived by stage from California for Rockwell—a finely tooled California saddle and a gallon of California's finest whiskey. It was said that Rockwell toasted many a drink to his young friend for remembering their ride together.

As his fame spread, Rockwell's role as a deputy marshal often required him to come to the aid of those in need. Whenever animals were stolen or other wrongs committed, citizens turned to Rockwell. In June 1869, a rancher named Nelson from Hamilton, Nevada, telegraphed Salt Lake City requesting Rockwell's help in finding ten valuable stolen horses and the men who had rustled them—two of Nelson's ranch hands. The horses were found, as reported in the *Hamilton Empire* and *Deseret News,* and in the end, all parties were satisfied except the rustlers.

In 1868, Herman Frances Reinhart woke up one morning at his camp near Stockton in Tooele County, only to find that fourteen of his horses had been stolen while he was asleep. Reinhart consulted with Brigham Young, who advised him to hire Porter Rockwell. Reinhart hesitated to do business with

Rockwell, as he had heard many rumors about Porter being a cold-blooded killer, but he wanted his horses back. So he sought out Porter, who made him an honest offer, or, as Reinhart put it, "Better than any other Gentile or white man." Rockwell offered to provide the supplies and horses for the search in return for two of Reinhart's horses when they were recovered. Reinhart accepted the offer. Before the search began, however, Reinhart got word that his horses were found near Fillmore, the thieves captured. Rockwell simply congratulated him on recovering his property and dropped the contract.

Another freighter named Alexander Toponce also hired Rockwell for his help. Toponce's eighteen oxen had been rustled. When he asked Rockwell if he could help, Rockwell laughed and said, "Your animals will be at your camp by tomorrow night." In fact, all eighteen oxen were back in camp the very next morning. When Toponce tried to thank Rockwell, Porter just laughed, declining payment for finding the slow-moving oxen.

SHOOT FIRST AND THEN INVITE THEM IN

PORTER OWNED A LOT OF PROPERTY, including a number of ranches. Among his hired hands was a young man by the name of Gudmundsen. He was on the ranch by himself protecting some of Porter's horses one night when he heard some men outside shouting at him to let them come in the cabin. Being young and naive, he poked his head out the door and called out, "Yes, come on in, I've got some coffee on." The next thing he knew, they were shooting at him.[49]

Gudmundsen dove into the cabin and blew out the candle while the three outlaws stole all of Porter's horses. When Porter arrived the next day, Gudmundsen told him what had happened.

---

49 John Rockwell has a picture of Gudmundsen as an old man telling his grandkids the story while his grandchildren stand at the doorway of the cabin and point at the bullet holes.

"You little fool," said Porter, only a little more coarsely. "You shoot first and then invite them in! That way they know you are armed."

Porter got back on his horse and took off in pursuit of the horse thieves. He arrived back at the ranch many hours later with all of his horses and the horses of the outlaws. But there were no other men with him.

"Mr. Rockwell, where are the horse thieves?" asked Gudmundsen.

All Porter would say was, "Last time I saw them they were facedown in a wash."

PORTER AND THE GUNSLINGERS

THE LEGEND OF PORTER'S HAIR and invulnerability proved an irresistible draw to gunslingers from all over the West who made their way to Salt Lake City to be the one to kill him, trying to disprove the notion of any divine protection. Unfortunately, there are no accounts from the men who made these attempts, since they all died trying. Here are a few stories recorded by onlookers.

SHOOTOUT ON LEHI STATE STREET

ONE OF THE WAYS TO GET famous in the Old West was to challenge a renowned gunslinger to a shootout. If you won, you gained instant celebrity. If you lost, it didn't matter to you anymore because you were dead. But the men who did the challenging never thought they'd lose.

Porter was confronted on State Street in Lehi one day by a young outlaw named Loren Dibble. Porter was not impressed, so he just stood there while Dibble emptied his gun shooting at him. Mind you, Dibble was a very good marksman, but every bullet missed.

When Dibble was out of ammunition, Porter took out two pistols and started firing at Dibble's feet, making him dance. When his pistols were empty, he put them back in his waistband and strode over to the frightened man and shook him like a rag doll while shouting at him, "If it wasn't for the fact that I know who your father really was, I'd have killed you," and then he threw him to the ground.[50]

---

50 Rockwell's cryptic comment about Dibble's parentage caused some in Lehi to spread the rumor that Dibble was a son of the Prophet Joseph Smith by plural marriage. Recently discovered information gives some validity to that effect.

Porter never explained how Dibble was able to fire at him repeatedly from a short distance without hitting him. The incident added to Porter's legend that his uncut hair and faithfulness was an absolute protection against bullet or blade.

CALIFORNIA GUNSLINGERS

A GROUP OF CALIFORNIA GUNSLINGERS got to talking one day, and they decided to make a wager in gold that whoever went to Utah and killed Porter Rockwell would get all the gold they had in the pot. One of them went to Utah, spied out Porter's daily schedule, and then found a good hiding spot at a place called Oak Hollow at the point of the mountain. When Porter came round the bend, this fellow stepped out on a horse with his pistol in hand and pointed it directly at Porter. Porter put his hands in the air.

Pleased with himself, the gunslinger told Porter about the bet and how much money he was going to win by killing him.

Always a quick thinker, Porter said casually, "You don't have a cap on your pistol—you can't kill me."

The startled outlaw dropped his gaze for just an instant to check his weapon, giving Porter time to throw his hand into his coat pocket where he kept his pistol. There wasn't time to draw, so Porter fired through his coat. He hit the outlaw in the heart, killing him on the spot.

Porter loaded the man into the back of his buckboard wagon, tied the man's horse to the back, and took the body back to Lehi, where he turned the body over to the local sheriff with an explanation of what had happened. The sheriff conducted a brief investigation, and Porter was cleared of any wrongdoing.

PORTER AND OATES

ONE OF THE MANY BUSINESS ventures that Porter started was a saloon and inn on the north side of the point of the mountain. It was an extremely profitable operation since it was ideally situated between Salt Lake City and Provo and on the route heading south to California.

Porter had a bartender working for him by the name of Hereford. One night, Porter was at the inn when he got in a fight with a freighter named Oates. Defending his boss, Hereford pulled a shotgun on Oates and told him to leave, which he did.

A little later that night, Porter announced that he had to get going because he wanted to go home to Lehi to spend the night, so he set out on the trail. As he worked his way around the point of the mountain, Oates confronted him with a bowie knife. When all was said and done, Oates's body was in the back of Porter's wagon being taken into Lehi, where it was turned over to the local official who conducted another investigation clearing Porter of wrongdoing.

JOE DORTON AND THE TONGUE OF FLAME

ON ANOTHER OCCASION, PORTER'S YOUNG employee Gudmundsen was asked to ride with Porter from Lehi to what is now Fairfield and Cedar Fort. About halfway there, a fellow named Joe Dorton had a little dugout in the hill from which he carried on trade with the soldiers at Camp Floyd.

Dusk was approaching when Porter went up to the door of the dugout to inquire of Joe about an outlaw he was tracking. The sought-after outlaw himself came to the door of the dugout when Porter knocked.

As Gudmundsen would later tell his family and record, the next thing he saw was Porter backing away from the door with his hands in the air while the outlaw pulled the trigger on his pistol. Gudmundsen testified that in the dark he saw a tongue of flame leap out of the barrel of the gun and said it looked as if the flames of the pistol were going right through Porter's chest and out his back. But incredibly Porter was completely unharmed.

When the man's gun was empty, he threw it on the ground and ran up the hill behind the house. Porter came over to the wagon, took out his rifle, and shot and killed the robber. He went over to the body and threw it down a dry well.[51]

---

51 The stories that involve Gudmundsen were in his unpublished diary. A handwritten copy by a member of the Gudmundsen Family was given to John W. Rockwell, which contains the above stories.

TALL TALES

THERE ARE SOME STORIES ABOUT Porter Rockwell that are simply too far-fetched to believe. One recurring story has Porter in a saloon somewhere when somebody calls him out. Porter stands calmly and lets the man shoot at him, and then Porter shakes his coat as all the lead bullets fall harmlessly to the floor.

Another story is told in the same vein but with the variation that someone calls Porter out and then pulls the trigger, only to have the gun misfire on every attempt, at which point the fellow drops the gun and runs out, never to be seen again.

One that sounds more credible is that two professional gamblers came into Salt Lake City to open a gambling den, with all its usual trappings. Porter knew the men by reputation. He finally confronted them, ordering them out of town, but they made it clear they had no intention of leaving with the large profits to be made fleecing the soldiers at Camp Douglas. Porter chose not to pursue the matter any further at that time. Around midnight, Porter walked to the Colorado Stables, which he owned, and was confronted by the two gamblers. The two men went for their guns and fired. Porter quickly aimed his double-barreled shotguns, pulling both triggers at once, and the two men were dead, while Rockwell was unharmed.

Another undocumented story has Porter looking for four outlaws when he got word that they were at the Utah-Colorado border. As the story goes, he loaded up his buckboard wagon with provisions and several bags of lime then headed off for his marks. When Porter finally confronted them, they resisted, resulting in four dead outlaws. To bring them back into Salt

Lake City for burial, Porter sat the four outlaws in the back of his buckboard, sitting up straight, tied together facing outward, with rifles in their hands. He poured lime over the outlaws, making them look like ghosts. He supposedly did this to frighten the Indians whose territory he would have to pass through.

Another odd story tells of Porter riding into a farmyard with pistol in hand, shooting the head off a chicken and telling the startled young boy in the farmyard, "Tell your ma that Porter Rockwell is here for dinner."

THE MCRAE BROTHERS

THERE ARE A FEW APOCRYPHAL stories about Rockwell arriving late at night at the front yard of a family with their dead son or sons in his buckboard. Whoever told these stories tried to portray a cruel streak in Porter that isn't evidenced in the documented stories.

One such story has Rockwell knocking on the door of a widow, her only son dead in the back of his wagon. Rockwell, with hat in hand, explained to the grief-stricken mother that her outlaw son refused to be taken alive.

Another story plays out about the same, except it's the father, who is a bishop at the time, who answers the door, and Rockwell berates the father, saying, "If you'd have raised your sons right, I wouldn't have had to kill them."

Though these stories are apocryphal, almost always lacking names and verifying details, there is one story that has names attached to it. In 1861, four highwaymen robbed a non-Mormon immigrant, John Love, of his money and his mule. Mr. Love identified the assailants as the McRae brothers, Kenneth and Alexander Jr., and the Manhard brothers, Charles and Truelove. A warrant was issued for the arrest of the four men. Within a few hours, the sheriff and his deputies closed in on the McRae brothers in Immigration Canyon.

The McRaes were ordered to surrender. What happened next is unclear, but in the end, the McRae brothers were dead.

The Manhard brothers, according to court records, were later imprisoned. Blame was laid on Rockwell by Samuel D. Sirrine for the killing of the two young outlaws and returning their dead bodies to the home of their parents.[52] It should be noted that their father, Alexander Sr., was a friend to Porter and also to Joseph Smith. During the Liberty Jail events, Alexander McRae Sr. was a fellow prisoner with Joseph, with Rockwell bringing them both food and helping in their attempts to escape. It is unlikely that Rockwell would have been the unnamed lawman who gunned down the two boys.

---

52 Samuel D. Sirrine. *The Destroying Angels of Mormondom; Or A Sketch of the Life of Orrin Porter Rockwell, the Late Danite Chief.* (San Francisco: Bancroft Library, 1887).

FAMILY, PRAYER, AND HEALING

PORTER LOVED HIS SECOND WIFE, Mary Ann, deeply and spent many happy years with her. But she eventually died in childbirth, leaving him alone once again. The baby died a short time later.

Several years later he married his housekeeper, Christina Olsen. She was a very practical and handy woman, who already knew and loved his children and who was accustomed to taking care of his household. Porter and Christina were sealed together by Brigham Young.

Porter and Christina had five children together, totaling fifteen children of his own with three wives and the adoption of two Indian children, William and Talitha. Brigham Young had asked the Saints to buy slaves from the Ute Indians whom they would otherwise sell into New Mexico and Mexico and to adopt these children and raise them as their own. Porter and Mary Ann accepted this request. Unfortunately, the two Indian children did not live long, one dying at twenty-one of tuberculosis, the other of brain fever at twenty-eight. Their lives with Porter and his family were almost certainly superior to what they would have experienced as slaves in the Southwest.

Porter had a spiritual side. George Washington Bean, in his diary, tells about the times he and Porter worked with the Indians, writing, "Porter was a very prayerful man, and we spent many hours teaching the Gospel to our . . . brethren." In fact, Brigham Young, while talking in a speech about relationships with the Indians said, "There's only one man whose opinion I trust when it comes to the Indians, and that's Porter's." He then went on to say that Porter had counseled him that the Mormons should live with the Indians, treat them as brethren, educate them, and live in peace with them. Perhaps that shows both a softer and more pragmatic side to Porter than he is usually given credit for.

Porter also defended women, as illustrated by an event that happened in Lehi. As a young man in Palmyra, New York, Porter witnessed Joseph Smith stop a man from being physically abusive to his wife. This made a deep impression on young Porter. Decades later, a young couple had made their home in Lehi. Porter apparently knew the bride and her parents. When he found out that her young husband was abusive to her, Porter talked with her to confirm the rumors. Then he showed up at their home in his wagon one morning, and the young woman came out with her baggage in hand and got into Porter's wagon. Her husband, standing at the door, wisely realized that he could do nothing to prevent his wife from leaving. Porter took the young woman back to her parents' home in Salt Lake, where she would be safe.

On another occasion, two men in the small town of Fountain Green, Utah, decided to take young plural wives. Since they each had sixteen-year-old daughters, they decided to make a trade, with each marrying the other's daughter. When one of the mothers discovered her husband's plans, she secretly packed up her daughter and shipped her off to Salt Lake to become Porter's new maid, where she knew she would be safe.

Regarding the gift of healing that Joseph Smith bestowed on Porter in his Mansion House blessing, there was a family named Sharp that lived out in Vernon, a small village in the west desert. Their baby boy, about two years old, came down with what was called summer fever and lay at death's door. Porter was working at his ranch over the mountain, about seventeen miles away. Knowing of his gift, the family sent someone to get Porter, but he didn't come. A bit later, the boy was even more seriously ill, so the family sent another person, but still Porter didn't come. Finally, toward evening, Porter rode up to the porch of the family's home.

Inside he found the mother at her wit's end, not knowing what else to do to save her child. "Why didn't you come?" she asked plaintively.

"I was busy and got here as soon as I could. So, what's wrong with the boy?

She told Porter, and he then asked, "Do you want your boy to live?

"Yes, with all my heart."

"Okay." Porter turned to the father and said, "Go out and bring me in the top cream from this morning's milking." Then he told the mother, "Bring me a loaf of bread and a bowl."

When all was assembled, Porter cut off a thick slice of bread and crumbled the bread into the bowl, then pouring the cream onto the bread. Using a spoon, he stirred the mixture then sat on a chair next to the boy's bed.

There was a young girl, perhaps eight or nine years old, named Esther Bennion, who was present when all this occurred, and she spoke of it many times throughout her life while teaching Primary class. In doing so she always called Porter by the title Elder Rockwell.

In relating the story she said, "I saw Elder Rockwell close his eyes, turn his head upward, and though no sound or words came out of his mouth, I could tell by the movements of his lips he was praying."

When he was through praying—a prayer that lasted at least five minutes, according to Sister Bennion—Porter took the spoon, stirred in the mixture, and rubbed the spoon over the boy's lips. He said, "Those are sore lips you have, let's see what God can do for them." Instantly the fever blisters disappeared. In a moment the boy woke up, and Porter began to feed the child some of the mixture.

While feeding the child, Porter said softly, "Now do you feel better? You get better and when you are older I will give you one of my colts out there at the ranch. I'll teach you how to shoot." The boy ate half the mixture, and Porter ate the rest. Porter then said, "Now go to sleep and when you wake you'll never know you've been sick, for you are well now."

When finished, Porter told the boy's mother, "Let him sleep through the night and by morning he'll be fine. This is what I do for my young ones when they get sick. He'll be fine."

As Porter arose and stepped out onto the porch, he found that many of the family's neighbors had gathered around to witness this miracle. Speaking to the crowd, he said, "This child is going to live to be an old man." He then began to point to different people in the group, saying things like, "Now you come in the morning and get the chores done." Pointing to another, "You take care of this evening's chores," and to a woman in the group, "You come over and fix breakfast for the family in the morning," and to another, "You come for lunch." Thus he healed the baby and made sure the family was taken care of.

The parents tried to thank Porter, but he stopped them and said, "Don't thank me. Give thanks to God, for He it was who saved your child's life. I deserve no credit." Then Porter left.

The boy lived to be eighty-seven years old.[53]

---

53 The information for this story comes from a letter to John W. Rockwell from Joanne Webber.

Porter As a Businessman

At his death in 1878, Rockwell's estate exceeded $40,000 in value, a handsome sum in that day. During his life, he had first tried farming as a youth. When he needed to make cash money quickly, he operated a ferry on the Big Blue River near Independence, Missouri. Finally, being sent to California by Brigham Young, Porter tried his hand at panning for gold but soon realized that he'd make more money catering to miners. So he opened up the Round Tent Saloon and two halfway houses, or hotels, in the California gold fields. After making money there, he would eventually return to Utah, and with the coming of Johnston's army and their settling at Camp Floyd, Rockwell opened up a hotel and brewery at the point of the mountain that he named the Hot Springs Brewery Hotel. He brewed beer and whiskey to sell to the travelers going through the area. He even sold his whiskey to mining camps, all the way into Montana. Many a Gentile and Mormon dignitary spent an evening at his hotel, including soldiers and officers from the army camp, and even Brigham Young and other Mormon leaders.

He eventually decided to get into ranching, and he and other men began to search the west desert for the best place to run cattle and horses. Porter selected the south end of Skull Valley at a place called Government Creek to raise horses and cattle. One of the Apostles at the time, Wilford Woodruff, wrote about Porter's fine ranch and how he had laid it out along Government Creek. Porter eventually would own all the land from Skull Valley south and then east to the Little Sahara sand dunes near Eureka, Utah. The value of that vast tract of land today is almost incalculable.

Later, Porter and Brigham Young decided to go into specialized horse breeding, and they had ordered horses from far away, probably Peru. These were very sturdy horses, with the ability to travel long distances. These horses were called horned horses because of a very unique feature—above each eye they had a tuft of hair that grew into a swirl looking like a tiny horn. Porter's horses were mostly thoroughbreds. He purchased injured thoroughbred mares from Wells Fargo and then bred them with wild mustang stallions he captured on the west desert, producing a fine line of horses. He also eventually bought the Colorado Stables in Salt Lake City, at the corner of Broadway and Main.

Later in life, many of the horses he had were white and were known as the white angel band. Old-timers clear into the Great Depression told stories of seeing remnants of the old white angel band still roaming the western deserts of Utah.

Rockwell was also successful in earning government mail contracts to deliver mail throughout parts of Utah.

PORTER'S LAST DAY

A T SIXTY-FIVE YEARS OLD, PORTER appeared to be in great health. He'd lived a hard life on the frontier, but he was still a powerfully built man at this age. On Saturday evening, June 8, 1878, Porter had tickets to the play *Joshua Whitcomb* at the Salt Lake Theater, staring famed actor Denman Thompson. Porter always enjoyed the theater and had twice tried his hand at acting. The first occasion was in Nauvoo when he played the part of the old Spanish soldier Davila in Joseph Smith's favorite play, *Bizarro*. When he reprised the role in Salt Lake City many years later, however, he forgot his line. He was supposed to get into an argument with another actor on the stage and then take out a dagger and bury it in his chest. But he forgot what he was supposed to say, and rather than wait for the prompter to give him his lines, he simply shouted out, "Do I stick him yet?" The audience burst into laughter, and that ended his acting career.

After attending the Salt Lake Theater that Saturday evening in June, he escorted his daughter home and then Porter did what he did quite often in the latter part of his life—he went to a nearby saloon and spent a few hours drinking. He would usually sit alone at a table, having a few drinks to spend the lonely hours of the evening. Sometimes he'd buy a round for the other patrons of the bar. His drinking didn't seem to bother any folks, since he was apparently the only person who was allowed to ride up and down Main Street roping signs off of stores after he'd a few too many. He could get away with that,[54] although he

---

54 He did not get away with riding his horse into the front door of a hotel, up the stairs, around the mezzanine, and then back down the stairs, and out the front door. He had to pay a fine for that one.

always took care to have the signs returned to their proper place when he sobered up.

After a few hours at the saloon, he retired to his office at the Colorado Stables there on Main Street. During the night he became very ill. He described his illness to the holster who ran the livery stable and then went back to bed. The next day, Sunday, he remained in his bed all day. At 5:00 PM, he quickly got up, pulled his boots on, and then fell back onto the bed and died.

Because of his fame and notoriety, a coroner was summoned to perform an autopsy. Some suspected that he might have been poisoned at the saloon the night before, but the autopsy confirmed that he died of natural causes, a heart attack.

The family was called in from the west desert, and the funeral arrangements were made. An editorial writer in the *Salt Lake Tribune,* which was heavily anti-Mormon at the time, wrote,

> He killed unsuspecting travelers, whose booty was coveted by his prophet-master. He killed fellow Saints who held secrets that menaced the safety of their fellow criminals in the priesthood. He killed Apostates who dared to wag their tongues about the wrongs they had endured. And he killed mere sojourners in Zion merely to keep his hand in.[55]

The newspaper provided no concrete examples of its claims, no proof of Rockwell's alleged misdeeds, and no names of victims—just unsupported allegations.

His funeral at the LDS 14th Ward was attended by more than a thousand people. Elder Joseph F. Smith said in his eulogy, "Some say he was a murderer. Well, if he was, he was also a friend of Brigham Young and Joseph Smith, and today he's ushered into

---

55 Schindler, 2nd ed., 367–68.

a Celestial Glory and apostates can go to Hell." Elder Smith went on to say, "He had his little faults, but Porter's life on earth, taken altogether, was one worthy of example, and reflected honor upon the Church. Through all the trials he has never once forgotten his obligations to his brethren and his God."

Looking back on Porter Rockwell's life, whom should history believe—Elder Smith or the 1878 *Salt Lake Tribune* editorial?

AFTERWORD

DAVID NORTON JR., MY GREAT-GREAT-GREAT-GRANDFATHER, was an associate of Porter Rockwell's from the earliest days of the Church. In fact, they both played a key role in the destruction of the *Nauvoo Expositor*: Porter kicked the door in, and David set the printing equipment on fire. They acted under orders of Mayor Joseph Smith, never suspecting that this act would ultimately lead to Joseph Smith's martyrdom.

After joining the Church in 1831, David taught the gospel to his Quaker neighbors, the Hammers, who joined the Church a few years later. The two families were close to each other and moved to Haun's Mill by 1838, just in time for the infamous Haun's Mill massacre. David Norton Jr. had a dream the night before the massacre, which prompted him to stay away from the mill that day, but Austin Hammer and his brother-in-law were killed at the mill.

After the massacre, David Jr. bought land south of Nauvoo but soon rented a place in town just a block away from Joseph Smith's home, which made him and Porter Rockwell neighbors. John Norton, David's oldest son, became a blacksmith, and my great-great-grandfather Wiley became a stonemason. After Joseph Smith was martyred, the Nortons went west with the Saints. John and Wiley married the two oldest Hammer girls near Winter Quarters. Brigham Young asked the two boys to join his vanguard company but excused Wiley because his wife was expecting. When Wiley and his young family got to the valley, he became a lawman with instructions to watch over the non-Mormons. Later, after helping in the conversion of a man who was on his way to the California gold fields, Brigham asked David and Wiley to go to the gold fields themselves to earn some cash for the Church. Wiley left his wife and young family to go to California as assigned.

As noted earlier in the book, Brigham Young sent Porter to collect tithing funds from Sam Brannon—a failed attempt because of Brannon's poor character. But Porter stayed in California and eventually owned at least three hotel-saloons in the California gold country. He needed someone he could trust to run these enterprises, and records from El Dorado, California, list Porter Rockwell as a hotel owner and David Norton Jr. as an innkeeper. It is almost a sure thing that David ran Porter's hotel in that village.

Upon returning to Utah, David Jr. joined the former branch president of Haun's Mill in founding Lehi, Utah. His sons John and Wiley built homes there during the Walker War of 1853 and helped build the fort.

Norton family histories contain accounts that suggest that Wiley Borrowman was the first sheriff of Salt Lake, but it was really James Ferguson (who came back from California in the same group as John Borrowman) who was the first sheriff of record. But what is clear is that Wiley was a deputy marshal, and therefore an associate of Porter Rockwell in law enforcement.

Thus, the Nortons and the Rockwells were associates from the beginning of the Church. Now two of us have reunited to tell the remarkable story of Porter Rockwell and his very singular life. It's fascinating how the circle closes. My brother Wayne Borrowman has researched the Norton and Hammer family line extensively and is the source of this information.

—Jerry Borrowman

ABOUT THE AUTHORS

JOHN W. ROCKWELL HAS SPENT his life teaching students history, especially U.S. history and history of the Wild West. He taught in Duchesne, Utah, and then in Taylorsville, Utah, at Eisenhower Junior High and Taylorsville High School for most of his career. He received the Distinguished Faculty Award from the National Honor Society in 2008. John has also worked on the Lehi City Historical Preservation Commission and has been involved in historical restoration and preservation projects throughout Lehi, Utah. John served an LDS mission in Mexico and has followed in his ancestor Porter's footsteps with lifelong service in the Church. A skilled marksman, he often competes in tournaments.

JERRY BORROWMAN IS AN AWARD-WINNING author of World War II coauthored biographies, including *Three Against Hitler* with Rudi Wobbe and *A Distant Prayer* with Joseph Banks. He's also a best-selling fiction writer, having written the popular four-book series starting with the World War I novel *'Til the Boys Come Home,* and the Depression-era novel *One Last Chance.* *Stories from the Life of Porter Rockwell* is his first writing outside the twentieth century, which opened a whole new world to his writing and to his own pioneer family. He is pleased to help John Rockwell turn a lifetime of research into a book. Jerry and Marcella are the parents of four children: Scott and his wife, Hilary; Jeff and his wife, Eden; Steven, and Kelissa.

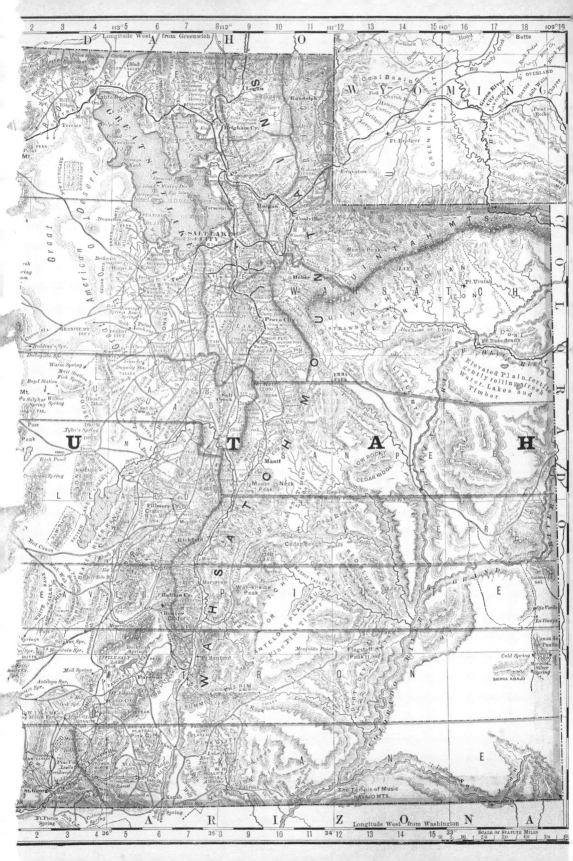

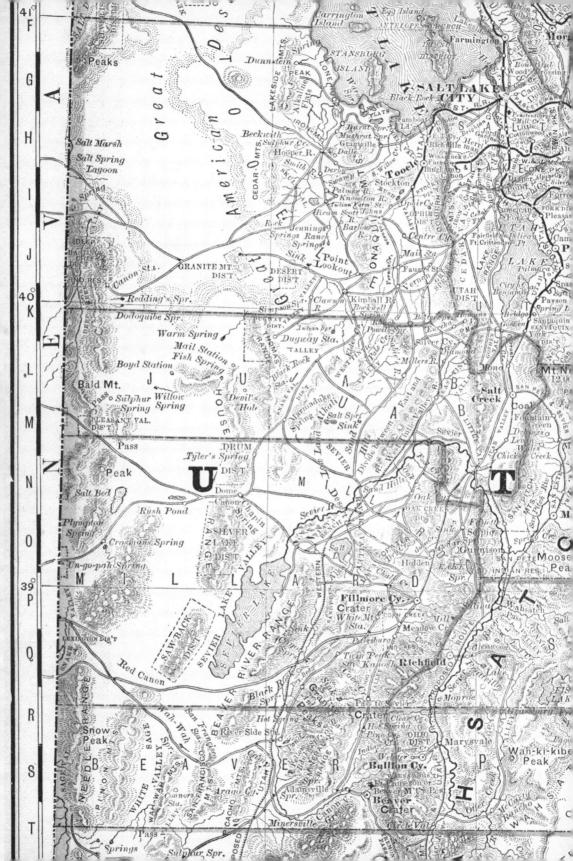